D1261179

The Philosophy of the Enlightenment

By the same author

The Hidden God

The Philosophy of
the Enlightenment

The Christian Burgess
and the Enlightenment

Lucien Goldmann

Translated by

Henry Maas

The MIT Press
Cambridge, Massachusetts

Originally published in 1968 as
Der christliche Bürger und die Aufklärung
© *1968 by Hermann Luchterhand Verlag GmbH*
First published in Great Britain in 1973
by Routledge & Kegan Paul Ltd
English translation © *Routledge & Kegan Paul Ltd 1973*
First MIT Press edition, 1973

Library of Congress catalog card number: 70 39648

ISBN: 0 262 07060 x

Printed in Great Britain

Contents

CONTENTS

Translator's Note

This essay was written in German and first published in 1968 under the title *Der christliche Bürger und die Aufklärung*. A French version (by Irène Petit) entitled *La Philosophie des Lumières* was included in Lucien Goldmann's collection of essays *Structures mentales et création culturelle* (Paris, 1970). This translation follows the original German text, incorporating further matter from the French edition and some additional corrections.

Preface

The following essay was originally written in 1960, in response to a commission from a German publisher, as the chapter on 'The Enlightenment and Christianity' in a projected history of Christian thought. In the event the book did not appear, and the publisher restored the copyright to me.

But for the original commission I should probably never have written on the Enlightenment, and certainly not without lengthy research. I should also have given less space to the relation between it and Christianity.

None the less the manuscript, such as it is, possesses a certain interest and may be worth publishing so long as the reader understands how it came into being. Perhaps, too, he may feel that I have compensated for the lack of scholarly research to some extent by developing certain hypotheses that I should hardly have ventured to advance in a more substantial work.

L.G.

Paris, May 1967

1 *The Structure of the Enlightenment*

The Encyclopédie

Eighteenth-century France is the country of the Enlightenment in its most fully developed and most thorough form; and the *Encyclopédie* directed by d'Alembert and Diderot is both a kind of symbol and a programme for the whole movement.

The *Encyclopédie* was of course only a part of a wider intellectual movement, and many important thinkers of the Enlightenment, including Voltaire, Rousseau, Helvétius and d'Holbach, made only occasional small contributions or none at all. None the less they maintained close links with the group that produced the *Encyclopédie* and though there are major differences between them, these concerned limited areas of their thought but not the idea itself of the *Encyclopédie* as central to the movement.

The *Encyclopédie* does not stand alone but is merely the best-known and largest undertaking of a whole series, from Bayle's *Dictionnaire historique et critique* to Voltaire's *Dictionnaire philosophique*. But if the *Encyclopédie* is specially representative of the movement, that is because both the contents themselves and the principles on which they are arranged express two leading features of the fundamental ideas of the Enlightenment:

(a) the great importance attached to making knowledge as comprehensive as possible;

(b) the idea that this knowledge is a *sum* of items of information to be conveyed in alphabetical order.

These of course are only approximations, and greater precision is needed if we are to avoid confusion. The writers of the Enlightenment always thought of knowledge in close connection with action. But they regarded human practice (*Praxis*), both in its effects on nature and in its social and historical consequences, as *individual* action, or the simultaneous action of individuals in large numbers, and as the application of knowledge acquired by the intellect. Knowledge, whether of nature or of society, is *autonomous*. Its existence and range depend on the practical experience of the individual; but it is not regarded as something whose content is determined by the collective action of mankind in history.

Thus human practice is seen as a socially important application of theoretical knowledge and moral principles. It is *not* seen as having an independent existence with the power to alter the content of knowledge and thus to bring about changes in human society. The thinkers of the Enlightenment in general lack all sense of the *dialectical* relation between knowledge and action, between self-awareness and practice.

The *philosophes* knew that the different fields of knowledge are interrelated, but this interrelation did not strike them as so fundamental as to make an internally organized presentation *indispensable* or *absolutely* preferable to the dictionary style of arrangement of information in separate items.

For them, the mission of man, which gives meaning to his life, lies in the effort to acquire the widest possible range of autonomous and critical knowledge in order to apply it technologically in nature and, through moral and political action, to society. Furthermore, in acquiring his knowledge, man must not let his thought be influenced by any authority or any prejudice; he must let the content of his judgements be determined only by his own critical reason.

Kant

Kant, who adopted many of the basic ideas of the Enlightenment, and in some important respects went beyond them, began his essay *An Answer to the Question: What is Enlightenment?* with the words:

Enlightenment is man's emergence from his self-imposed minority. This minority is the inability to use one's own understanding without the guidance of another. It is self-imposed if its cause lies not in a lack of understanding, but in the lack of courage and determination to rely on one's own understanding and not another's guidance. Thus the motto of the Enlightenment is 'Sapere aude! Have the courage to use your own understanding!' Idleness and cowardice are the reasons why so great a part of mankind, after nature has long since released them from the tutelage of others, willingly remain minors as long as they live; and why it is so easy for others to set themselves up as their guardians. It is most convenient to be a minor. If I have a book to reason for me, or a confessor to act as my conscience, or a physician to prescribe my diet, and so on, I need not take any trouble myself. As long as I can pay, I do not have to think. Others will spare me the tiresome necessity.

Needless to say, this attitude had already brought the Enlightenment into conflict with traditional Christianity. Any religion that depends on revelation must insist that perception and reason cannot suffice to give man the knowledge he needs in all the important questions of life; such knowledge requires correction, or at any rate needs to be supplemented by knowledge resting on the authority of revelation.

The *philosophes* were of course well aware that human knowledge has its limits. The difference between their attitude and the religious one lies not in their assuming that human thought is omnipotent and able to penetrate to the essential nature of things, but rather in the fact that they considered human reason, based on sense-perception, able to reach positive results in a whole range of questions fundamental to human life, results standing in no need of correction by faith; from this view the more radical thinkers of the Enlightenment, especially in France, proceeded to

3

the assertion that the human intellect is capable of obtaining such results in *all* essential questions. If this is so, all knowledge given by revelation becomes superfluous, deceptive, and, in Kant's phrase, dangerous to human adulthood.

Kant continues:

> I set the central achievement of Enlightenment—that is, of man's emergence from his self-imposed minority—above all in matters of religion. I do so because our rulers take no interest in playing the guardian to their subjects in matters of art and science. Besides, this religious dependence is both the most damaging and the most humiliating of all.

Later in this essay which we have taken as our point of departure, Kant declares that it is vital to Enlightenment not merely that men should free their thinking from all authority, but also that they should make free *public* use of their reason, and that all should have unfettered rights to report the results of their thought in speech and writing.

On the other hand, Kant tells us, there may be practical limitations to this right that present no difficulties to Enlightenment 'but are actually favourable to it'. These are limitations on the 'private use' that the individual may make of his reason in a civic capacity or *public* appointment.

The particular tone of Kant's essay is of course determined by the concrete social and political situation in Germany in his time, and by the weakness of the middle class, as a result of which the German Enlightenment was necessarily much less radical than, for example, the French. The leading French thinkers could hardly have admitted the existence of such a division between thought and action. In pointing it out, Kant revealed one of the great weaknesses of the movement—even though he himself did not think it one. He is confirmed by the fact that any difficulties encountered by the *philosophes* came purely from the publication of their writings; they in no way resulted from any attempt to apply their ideas to their own professional activities. This is well illustrated by the case of Jean Meslier. In the eyes of his parishioners his career was that of a model priest, never touched by the least suspicion of heterodoxy or atheism; yet after his death he was found to have written one of the most radically anti-Christian and atheistic books of the time, and its publication caused an immense uproar.

This divorce between thought and action seems to reflect one of the basic ideas of the French Enlightenment—the notion that the unhampered advance of knowledge and general education would suffice, without any further action, to bring about the liberation of mankind and to end the great social evils of the day.

Dialectical criticism

Hegel The Enlightenment—taking the word in the broadest sense as the individualist vision of the world, whether rationalist or empirical or composite and intermediate[1]—is one of the four important forms of thought[2] in the modern history of western civilization.

It has become usual in our day to accept the German idealist view of the Enlightenment as a limited type of thought largely superseded by the three other great world visions—the tragic, the romantic and the dialectical. There is some justification, it is true, in the dialectical critique and in criticism from the religious point of view generally; but it is my thesis that these criticisms need some revision in the light of twentieth-century experience.

As a preliminary step I shall outline the dialectical critique, and then give a general account of the Enlightenment as a whole.

The dialectical critique is most effectively expressed in the two outstanding works of dialectical philosophy, Hegel's *Phenomenology of Mind* and Goethe's *Faust*.

Hegel begins his chapter on the Enlightenment (*Phenomenology*, 'Spirit in self-estrangement', section two; translation by J. A. Baillie) by asserting that the great theme of the Enlightenment is

---

[1] 'Composite and intermediate' describes most of the thinkers usually considered in France as the Enlightenment in the narrower sense.

[2] The three others are: the *tragic*, in Pascal and Kant; the *romantic*; the *dialectical*, in Hegel and Marx.

the struggle against religion: 'The peculiar object on which pure insight directs the active force of the notion is belief.' But he adds at once that because of the change in human consciousness at this stage of historical development (a Marxist would say, because of the rise of the bourgeoisie and its rationalist type of thought) the Faith with which the Enlightenment was battling had shrunk to a mere body of knowledge about God, a 'science of God', as restricted in scope as the rationalist view opposing it. This is Hegel's meaning in speaking of belief as 'a form of pure consciousness like itself [pure insight, i.e. the Enlightenment] and yet opposed to it *in that element*'.[1]

The Enlightenment however is not merely the battle against a faith shrunk to superstition and 'science of God'. It is also a critical conception of the world, a way of seeing man's relation to the world in terms of rational knowledge, *pure insight*.

But at the same time pure insight has a relation to the actual world, for like belief it is a return from the actual world into pure consciousness. We have first of all to see how its activity is constituted, as contrasted with the impure intentions and the perverted forms of insight found in the actual world.

The Enlightenment appears first as the critical spirit, as 'pure ingenious thought' tearing down everything that stands, and so breaking and destroying itself.

The sphere of culture has itself rather the most painful feeling, and the truest insight about itself—the feeling that everything made secure crumbles to pieces, that every element of its existence is shattered to atoms, and every bone broken: moreover it consciously expresses this feeling in words, pronounces judgement and gives luminous utterance concerning all aspects of its condition.

The rationalist view, however, lacks the essential content of historical knowledge—knowledge of the *process* of historical

---

[1] My italics.

development itself, or (in Marxist rather than Hegelian terms) awareness of human development in history as a product of human action. It thus lacks the one content that can transform the nature of historical knowledge and change it from passive contemplation into active awareness, from knowledge of the object into consciousness of the human subject and awareness of the nature of human existence.

> Pure insight therefore can have no activity and content of its own, and thus can only take up the formal attitude of truly apprehending this ingenious insight proper to the world and the language it adopts.

If knowledge is inactive and lacks the essential historical content it is ineffective. The reality implied in it can be comprehended only in a perspective that transcends it. The implicit content of the Enlightenment is the systematic interpretation of nature and its technical application. It is the subsequent general diffusion of this knowledge that has contributed to the transformation of society and thus fulfilled a genuine historical function.

> Since this language is a scattered and broken utterance and the pronouncement a fickle mood of the moment, which is again quickly forgotten, and is only known to be a whole by a third consciousness, this latter can be distinguished as pure insight only if it gathers those several scattered traces into a universal picture, and then makes them the insight of all.

These words of Hegel's of course refer to the *Encyclopédie*. In the Enlightenment this is the real step forward towards effective action transcending purely theoretical knowledge. It is the first step taken on the road which, through the work of Diderot, leads to the awareness of content, which is the true activity of mind or (in Marxist terms) of man's consciousness of his historic role. The *Encyclopédie* was a collaborative enterprise which undertook to make a complete collection of knowledge, to make it available to all, and thus to advance from individualist 'parleying' to a historic whole.

By this simple means pure insight will resolve the confusion of this world. For we have found that the fragments and determinate conceptions and individualities are not the essential nature of this actuality, but that it finds its substance and support alone in the spirit which exists *qua* judging and discussing, and that the interest of having a content for this ratiocination and parleying to deal with alone preserves the whole and the fragments into which it falls. In this language which insight adopts, its self-consciousness is still particular, a self existing for its own sake; but the emptiness of its content is at the same time emptiness of the self knowing that content to be vain and empty. Now, since the consciousness placidly apprehending all these sparkling utterances of vanity makes a collection of the most striking and penetrating phrases [the *Encyclopédie*], the soul that still preserves the whole, the vanity of witty criticism, goes to ruin with the other form of vanity, the previous vanity of existence. The collection shows most people a better wit, or at least shows everyone a more varied wit than their own, and shows that better knowledge and judging in general are something universal and are now universally familiar. Thereby the single and sole interest which was still found is done away with; and individual light is resolved into universal insight.

In the *Encyclopédie* the unhistorical individualism of critical and intelligent reasoning found a means of historic expression adequate to its real nature. This expression was a collective one, both in the sense that the work was a collaborative production and in the variety of the social classes which it aimed to unite in a shared ideology.

But arrayed against the *Encyclopédie* there still stands faith, a faith superseded by history and inherently empty, a faith which has shrunk to a science of God. It is not so much the acquisition of knowledge and mastery over nature as the battle against faith that is the real historic activity of the Enlightenment. 'But above empty knowledge there still stands fast the knowledge of the essence, and pure understanding first appears in its proper role when it challenges faith.' The following section deals accordingly with the 'battle of the Enlightenment against superstition'.

Goethe In Goethe's *Faust* we encounter a similar point of view. The opening of the play pleasantly presents the conflict between the highest ideals of the Enlightenment and the real content of the new dialectical thinking. The old scholar whom we meet at the beginning of the first act exactly embodies the human ideal of the Enlightenment. But precisely because his knowledge (as befits a realization of this ideal) is encyclopedic, Faust has become aware of its limitations and of the need to pass beyond them to the reality of life.

The theme of the play is Faust's path from the confident, critical scholar and researcher to the man who discovers the real meaning of life, a meaning that Goethe, without being Christian himself, poetically represents as the way to God. It would be no exaggeration to say that Faust's first words exactly express the human ideal of the Enlightenment:

I've studied now Philosophy
And Jurisprudence, Medicine,—
And even, alas! Theology,—
From end to end, with labour keen.

> (Translation by Bayard Taylor)

Through his studies Faust, the scholar, has become more cultivated than ordinary people, freeing himself not only from Christianity but from all religion.

I'm cleverer, true, than those fops of teachers,
Doctors and Magisters, Scribes and Preachers;
Neither scruples nor doubts come now to smite me,
Nor Hell nor Devil can longer affright me.

But it is just this experience that has brought him to apply his critical approach to himself, to recognize the limits of pure

9

knowledge and perceive its fundamental inadequacy and emptiness. He has sought in vain for the real meaning of life, and now
he resorts to magic:

> No dog would endure such a curst existence!
> Wherefore from Magic I seek assistance,
> That many a secret perchance I reach
> Through spirit-power and spirit-speech,
> And thus the bitter task forego
> Of saying the things I do not know,—
> That I may detect the inmost force
> Which binds the world and guides its course;
> Its germs, productive powers explore,
> And rummage in empty words no more!

Pure knowledge now seems to him alien to life and the real
world:

> Ah, me! this dungeon still I see,
> This drear, accursed masonry,
> Where even the welcome daylight strains
> But duskly through the painted panes.
> Hemmed in by many a toppling heap
> Of books worm-eaten, gray with dust,
> Which to the vaulted ceiling creep,
> Against the smoky papers thrust,—
> With glasses, boxes, round me stacked,
> And instruments together hurled,
> Ancestral lumber, stuffed and packed—
> Such is my world: and what a world!
> And do I ask, wherefore my heart
> Falters, oppressed with unknown needs?
> Why some inexplicable smart
> All movement of my life impedes?
> Alas! in living Nature's stead,
> Where God His human creature set,
> In smoke and mould the fleshless dead
> And bones of beasts surround me yet!

Faust's resort to magic should not be understood as a romantic conversion from intellect to mysticism or from reason to the irrational. The spirits that he summons up in his invocation and with whom he talks are the representatives of the two great visions of the world whose clash provides the theme of the play, the highest form of rationalism, as embodied in the Enlightenment, the world vision of Spinoza, and the Dialectic, whose vision of man transcends all Enlightenment and every kind of rationalism. The two spirits, the Macrocosm and the Earth-Spirit, are embodiments of these two visions: pure intellect and historic action.

Spinoza was the first philosopher to use reason to reach awareness of totality, of the Whole, a concept that remained more or less foreign to all the individualist philosophers. For this reason his philosophy appeared to the dialectical thinkers and poets as the highest form of rationalism, as the extreme limit to which pure reason can go. Amor Dei Intellectualis, the intellectual love of God, a God identical with the world, the intellectual love of the Whole.

The initial impression made on Faust by the Macrocosm is overwhelming:

How each the Whole its substance gives,
Each in the other works and lives!
Like heavenly forces rising and descending,
Their golden urns reciprocally lending,
With wings that winnow blessing
From Heaven through Earth I see them pressing,
Filling the All with harmony unceasing!

But he immediately recognizes the limitations of pure knowledge:

How grand a show! but, ah! a show alone.
Thee, boundless Nature, how make thee my own?
Where you, ye breasts? Founts of all Being, shining,
Whereon hang Heaven's and Earth's desire,
Whereto our withered hearts aspire,—
Ye flow, ye feed: and am I vainly pining?

Knowledge independent of historic action is perhaps accessible to God, but even in its highest form it can give man nothing essential, no content to fill his life. Accordingly Faust turns to the Earth-Spirit, whose essence is *action* (working for that reason in *time*, while Spinoza's rationalism creates a timeless picture of the universe):

> In the tides of Life, in Action's storm,
> A fluctuant wave,
> A shuttle free,
> Birth and the Grave,
> An eternal sea,
> A weaving, flowing
> Life, all-glowing,
> Thus at Time's humming loom 't is my hand prepares
> The garment of Life which the Deity wears!

Faust perceives that this message alone can reveal the meaning of life and the way to God:

> Thou, who around the wide world wendest,
> Thou busy Spirit, how near I feel to thee!

But the answer is shattering:

> Thou art like the Spirit which thou comprehendest,[1]
> Not me!

There is still an abyss between Faust and the Earth-Spirit, one that only a transformation of character can enable him to cross. Until he transcends his world vision, the pure scholar, the man of the Enlightenment, remains incapable of reaching beyond reason and intellect to the essence of life, historic action.

It is precisely the purpose of the play to present the crossing of this abyss: the course of a scholar of the Enlightenment from the spirit of knowledge, which he embodies at the beginning, to the spirit of action, which shows him the way to the Absolute, to God.

---

[1] 'Comprehend' is used deliberately. The passage is concerned precisely with the gap between pure 'comprehension' and historical 'action'.

Criticism of the Enlightenment reappears with the entry of Faust's assistant, Wagner, who represents the most limited form of the spirit of the Enlightenment. As he says, he has zealously devoted himself to study, acquired great knowledge, but still longs to know everything. His one anxiety is that life is too short for him to learn all he wants to know. For all his critical efforts, he often feels that 'in head and breast there's something wrong'.

How hard it is to compass the assistance
Whereby one rises to the source!

Like all the thinkers of the Enlightenment he would of course like to use his knowledge to direct the world, but he realizes that the possibility is remote:

Ah, when one studies thus, a prisoned creature,
That scarce the world on holidays can see,—
Scarce through a glass, by rare occasion,
How shall one lead it by persuasion?

This 'soulless sneak' understands nothing of Faust's invocation of the spirits. Hearing Faust speaking alone, he enters in dressing-gown and nightcap (symbol of an outworn creed), a light in his hand, in the belief that Faust is declaiming a Greek tragedy, an art from which he would gladly 'profit' (for a scholar is ceaselessly busy enlarging his culture).

It would, however, be wrong to think that Goethe saw only the negative side and the inadequacy of the Enlightenment. Once the problem is stated and the inadequacy made clear, two later scenes show—as Hegel does—the positive side of the movement. In the first, 'Before the city-gate', an old peasant expresses the people's gratitude to Faust for the skilled medical help he gave them during an outbreak of plague. The other is the scene in Part Two where Faust returns to his former laboratory. He encounters his old pupil, Wagner, who has taken his place, and carried on his work. He has earned the gratitude of the people, and become old, honoured and famous. He has advanced so far in scientific knowledge that he has succeeded in producing a synthetic human being, the Homunculus. Here too we can see the limits of pure knowledge. Wagner can bring the Homunculus to life, but he cannot control or direct him. Almost as soon as the Homunculus is living he prepares to go out into the world. When Wagner anxiously asks, 'And I?' the answer is:

> You
> Will stay at home, most weighty work to do,
> Unfold your ancient parchments.

As this study is devoted to the Enlightenment, I shall not continue the detailed analysis of *Faust*. It is clear enough from what has been said that its theme is the replacement of the Enlightenment by the discovery of historic action, which is represented as the only way to God. One further scene may be quoted, since it makes the point particularly clear. Faust, left alone after Wagner's departure, and shattered by the Earth-Spirit's rejection of him, is on the point of suicide when the message of the Easter bells stays his hand. The lines are famous:

> Why, here in dust, entice me with your spell,
> Ye gentle, powerful sounds of Heaven?
> Peal rather there, where tender natures dwell.
> Your messages I hear, but faith has not been given;
> The dearest child of Faith is Miracle.
> I venture not to soar to yonder regions
> Whence the glad tidings hither float;
> And yet, from childhood up familiar with the note,
> To Life it now renews the old allegiance.

'Your messages I hear, but Faith has not been given.' The philosophy of the Enlightenment was critical and anti-Christian. It had not merely turned faith into superstition; it had lost the capacity to feel the content of religion altogether, above all the content of Christianity. The bells seem to ring only for 'tender natures' (*weiche Menschen*), i.e. for the common people.

Though Faust leaves the ideal of the Enlightenment behind him, he does not become a Christian. But he does recover the capacity to understand the content of religion and its meaning for men; he perceives the need for an answer to the religious questions to which the Enlightenment completely closed its eyes. That is why the Easter bells are able to call him back to life, a life in which he can find the true meaning of the message. That meaning is action, which restores the reality of God and the Devil. Through the pact with the Devil, and *only* through this pact, action opens up man's way to God.

The economic and social background

This critique of the Enlightenment by Hegel and Goethe is frequently echoed by later writers, though less sympathetically and with a less comprehensive grasp. Its purpose was to emphasize the essential problem of the relation between knowledge and historic action, between the Enlightenment and the Dialectic. After our brief sketch of it, the next task is to examine the nature of the knowledge with which the Enlightenment was concerned, or, more precisely, the fundamental categories determining its content.

We have long since learned from the social history of ideas that *every* mode of human thought and feeling is determined by mental structures which are closely related to the objective life of the particular society in which they develop. For this reason it is not enough for a modern scientific study of an intellectual movement to catalogue its still valid achievements and its limitations. The effort must be made to ground them in the general categorical structure of the movement if we are to understand the factors making the achievements possible and the limits inescapable.

In the whole history of ideas there are few subjects that have been so often or so thoroughly treated as the Enlightenment. But although there are good monographs on particular aspects of the movement, no satisfactory comprehensive study has yet been produced.

There are two main reasons for this. First (with one exception, to be discussed later) the modern method of genetic and structural investigation has not been applied to the Enlightenment. An undertaking of this sort would take years of detailed research, so that in this essay it will barely be possible to do more than formulate some provisional general hypotheses, offered at the most as a starting-point for further research.

The second reason is that most of the leading books on the Enlightenment were written in a period ruled by values which the experience of western society in our time has forced us to question. When we speak of the Enlightenment and Christianity, the events of the past thirty years have made much that earlier passed as obviously true look very different now.

With these reservations, the territory of the subject may now be delimited. In the field of intellectual history there can of course be no such precise definitions as in the natural sciences. There are no classes to be defined by particular characteristics belonging to all their members and to nothing else. The scientific history of ideas is a structural and genetic description combining analysis and exposition. It can claim scientific exactness only when the analysis is sufficiently detailed.

It follows that a study of the Enlightenment must give not only a structural account of the movement as a whole, but must also reveal the structural organization of its various tendencies. This attempt has frequently been made at the empirical level, and it cannot on this occasion be raised to the level of a scientific study. None the less something, at least by way of hypothesis on the essential nature of Enlightenment thought, may be suggested now.

The accepted meaning of 'the Enlightenment' includes the various rationalist and empirical currents of thought of eighteenth-century Europe, especially France and England. In the perspective of intellectual history, these currents have their origins in earlier centuries, while their development has continued into our own time. On the other hand, as Hegel pointed out, and as Groethuy-sen fully demonstrated in his excellent book, there was a fundamental relation between the anti-Christian philosophers of the Enlightenment and those eighteenth-century thinkers who, for example in France, defended Christianity against the attacks of the Enlightenment.

In the perspective of social history the Enlightenment is a historically important stage in the development of western bourgeois thought, which, as a whole, constitutes a unique and vital part of human intellectual history. To understand the essential ideas of the Enlightenment, one must accordingly start by analysing the activity that was most important to the bourgeoisie and most influenced its social and intellectual evolution. This was the development of the economy, and above all its essential element, exchange.

In sociological terms, the history of the bourgeoisie is primarily economic history. The word is used here in a narrow sense, in which there is not an 'economy' in all human societies, at all times and in all places; it is used only of those groups in which the production and distribution of goods are not in any way controlled—no matter whether the control is rational, authoritarian, religious or traditional. Thus there is no economy in this sense in a medieval peasant family growing food for its own consumption, nor on a feudal estate living on its own produce and on natural abundance obtained without cultivation, nor in a large-scale system of planning like that of the present-day Soviet Union. In all these instances the commodities are produced and distributed—fairly or unfairly, in humane or barbarous manner—on principles governed by the *use-value* and actual qualities of the goods.

An economy in our sense exists only where economic activity is not governed by the use-value of the goods produced—the *use* of the goods to people, individually or socially—but by the possibility of selling the goods on the market and realizing their *exchange-value*.

Now as the organization of production and distribution based on exchange-value develops within the previously established framework of production and comes to supersede it, a progressive change in the people's manner of life and thought sets in. It is not easy to list the main features of this process of change, as the causally determined historical order in which they appear does

17

not correspond with the systematic arrangement of their essential qualities. As the present work is not historical, we shall adopt a systematic enumeration and begin with a characteristic that appears on the surface only in developed exchange economies but forms the basis of all the others, and thus offers a direct means of making the intellectual history of the western European bourgeoisie comprehensible.

The autonomy of the individual The most important consequence of the development of a market economy is that the individual, who previously constituted a mere partial element within the total social process of production and distribution, now becomes, both in his own consciousness and in that of his fellow men, an independent element, a sort of monad, a *point of departure*. The social process of course continues and implies a certain regulation of production and exchange. This process was not only objectively present in the earlier social structure but also *consciously realized* in the traditional, religious and rational rules governing people's behaviour; these rules now begin to fade from consciousness. The regulation of the market is now *implicit*, governed by the blind forces of supply and demand. The total social process is seen as resulting mechanically and independently of the individual will from the action of countless autonomous individuals on each other and in response to each other, behaving as rationally as possible for the protection of their private interests and basing their actions on their knowledge of the market with no regard for any trans-individual authority or values.

It was thus inevitable that the development of a market economy, starting as early as the thirteenth century, should progressively transform western thought. This development seems to be the social foundation of the two great world visions characteristic of the European outlook, that dominated it up to the time of Pascal, of Kant, and even longer, and have persisted alongside the tragic, the romantic and the dialectic visions. They are the rationalist and the empirical traditions, and their synthesis, the French Enlightenment.

At first glance rationalism and empiricism seem to be so opposed in their philosophical approach, and to give such opposite answers to every philosophical question, that one may well ask how they can possibly both be derived from the development of the bourgeoisie, and how most of the eighteenth-century writers of the Enlightenment in France managed without any special difficulty to adopt a position half-way between the two extremes.

The answer seems to be that these two philosophies share the same fundamental concept: the treatment of the individual consciousness as the *absolute origin* of knowledge and action. Pure rationalism finds this origin in clear innate ideas existing independently of experience; pure empiricism, rejecting entirely the notion of innate ideas, finds the origin in sense-perceptions more or less mechanically organized into conscious thought.

The majority of the thinkers of the French Enlightenment occupied a third position, intermediate between rationalism and empiricism. They were sharply anti-Cartesian, laughed at Descartes' physics (his 'romance of vortices', as they called it) and found their great examples in Newton and Locke, denying, with the latter and all the empiricists, the existence of innate ideas, and holding that individual consciousness is invariably based on experience. None the less they generally acknowledged, expressly or by implication, the active role of reason in collecting the knowledge which has been acquired through perception and preserved in the memory, organizing it in the form of thought and science, and directing action, under the influence of feeling, towards the greatest satisfaction and happiness of the individual.

For all the differences between these three philosophical systems, it is none the less clear that we have before us three forms of the same individualism, and that the temporary dominance of one form or another was determined largely by the objective social situation in different countries at different times.[1]

---

[1] See my *Mensch, Gemeinschaft und Welt in der Philosophie Immanuel Kants* (Europa Verlag, Zürich, 1946).

It seems self-evident that there is a close relation between the development of the market economy, in which every individual appears as the autonomous source of his decisions and actions, and the evolution of these different philosophical visions of the world, all of which treat the individual's consciousness as the absolute origin of his knowledge and action. Likewise, the disappearance from human consciousness of all trans-individual authority regulating production and distribution is matched by the fundamental claim of all the writers of the Enlightenment that individual reason must be recognized as the supreme arbiter and subjected to no higher authority.

This is by no means the only relation between the Enlightenment and the bourgeoisie. All the fundamental categories of Enlightenment thought have a basic structure analogous to that of the market economy, which constitutes in its turn the social basis of the evolving bourgeoisie. It will be enough to mention the most important of them.

Contract Every act of exchange requires the participation of at least two parties. There is a set abstract relation between them which may be defined as follows: the agreement of two autonomous individual wills creates a mutually binding engagement; this engagement may be altered only if a new agreement is made, or if it is proved that the will of either of the parties was not autonomous at the time of the agreement, as a result either of deception (causing a hindrance to knowledge) or of physical constraint (restricting action). This relation is inherent in every act of exchange and constitutes the sole interpersonal relation implied by the transaction. This is the relation of *contract*.

It is natural enough, then, that all individualist thinkers, and particularly those of the Enlightenment, should think of society as a contract between large numbers of autonomous individuals combining to establish a community, a nation, a state. The contract is the basic mental category in which the Enlightenment thought of human society and especially the state. We meet this concept in a succession of entirely diverse thinkers stretching from Hobbes and Locke to Grotius and Diderot, and above all in Rousseau's *Social Contract*.

Equality This is the place to ask why Rousseau's concept of the social contract put all others into the background; why, since its publication, other versions of the theory have been relegated to academic study.

The answer to this question lies in the historical and political ideas of the Enlightenment. For the moment we may say that most of the other theories of social contract, both those deriving from seventeenth-century politics and those originating in the Enlightenment's preference for monarchy in the eighteenth century, regarded the social contract as a contract establishing the state by the *subjection* of its members. Rousseau, by contrast, saw the contract from the start as bound up with the other basic value of the Enlightenment, that of equality. In his view the social contract is an agreement between *free* and *equal* individuals, all undertaking to put themselves entirely under the general will. The essence of the social contract is defined thus: 'Each of us puts his person and all his power in common under the supreme direction of the general will, and, in our corporate capacity, we receive each member as an indivisible part of the whole' (Book I, chapter 6).

The social contract creates the general will in which 'all citizens are equal' (Book III, chapter 6), and the general will then determines the form of government.

Furthermore Rousseau was the first to relate (though only in abstract terms) the theory of social contract with the distinction between the individual will and the general will. (This distinction becomes fundamental in Hegel and Marx in the analysis of the private and state spheres of social life, and of their relations in modern society.)

To continue our analysis of the act of exchange: the transaction of course postulates *equality* between the parties as an essential condition of the contract. However great the differences in rank or wealth that distinguish them in the rest of their social life, in the act of exchange, as sellers and buyers of goods (also when the goods are in the abstract form of money), the parties to the transaction are strictly equal. The act of exchange is essentially *democratic*. Needless to say, its democratic element is purely formal, and implies nothing as to the real content of the exchange. (This is why the Marxist critique of formal democracy fastens chiefly on a privileged act of exchange, the sale and purchase of human labour.) But within the framework of the transaction all economic distinctions between the parties are disregarded. The equality of all actual and potential parties to a contract is a fundamental condition of its mere existence.

Universality   Next, exchange generates the idea of *universality*. The buyer uses the market to find a seller, and vice versa, but is not concerned with the personal character of the other. In principle, if the conventions of the exchange are sufficiently developed, the behaviour of the parties towards each other is fixed by general rules completely independent of who the parties actually are.[1] Thus the category of universality (which is implicit in any catalogue offering goods for sale at stated prices to any customer) increasingly becomes the effect as well as the condition of the exchange of goods.

Toleration   A fourth category of thought which is both produced by exchange and furthers its development is *toleration*. It is hardly necessary to justify the assertion. Exchange entirely disregards the religious and moral convictions of the parties just as it disregards their other objective qualities. These convictions are irrelevant to the act of exchange, and it would be absurd to take them into account. Whether the other party is a Christian, Jew or Mohammedan makes no difference to his ability to transact the exchange validly. This analysis is confined also by the historical fact that the development of commercial relations has always worked against fanaticism and wars of religion.

[1] This of course is valid only for a liberal economy and not for a monopoly economy, in which elements of collective planning are beginning to appear.

Freedom We now come to the two most important categories which, like the others, are both the condition and the result of the development of exchange: freedom and property.

Exchange is possible only between parties that are equal and free. Any restriction on freedom of will or action automatically destroys the possibility of an act of exchange. A slave or serf cannot of course sell his possessions on his own account. On the other hand it is unthinkable for a merchant, every time he makes a sale or purchase, to be obliged to inquire into the previous life or civil status or rights of his client. This problem arose in a concrete form in the twelfth and thirteenth centuries at the high point of the agricultural period of the European economy, when the towns were beginning to develop; and it brought legal complications in its train. The commercial activity which provided the foundation of the newly growing towns was very frequently held back by the feudal structure of the countryside. For example, it became increasingly difficult to accept that purchases or sales made in the town could suddenly be declared null and void simply because the client was a runaway serf who did not possess the right to buy or sell. As a result special laws were enacted for market days, the *jus fori*, and in this way the towns began to gain their freedom, though often only after a long and bitter struggle. This freedom is implied in the words 'There is freedom in town air', meaning that in general all trace of previous serfhood could be eliminated by the acquisition of citizenship of a town or sometimes merely by sufficiently long residence within its boundaries.

Property Lastly, an exchange can take place only if the two parties have rights of disposal over the goods they intend to exchange, or, more precisely, if they enjoy the unlimited rights of ownership under the law of *jus utendi et abutendi*.

With this we conclude the list of the principal mental categories necessary to the development of a society founded on exchange, categories which also acted to further its development: individualism, entailing the disappearance of all trans-individual authority; the contract, forming the basis of all human relations; equality; universality; toleration; freedom; property.

Ethical theory

Anyone who knows the eighteenth century in France will see that this list (and it is no coincidence) is identical with the fundamental categories of the thought of the Enlightenment.

Whatever differences there were in other respects between the philosophers of the Enlightenment, these categories (with a few exceptions, to which we shall return) were accepted by the majority of them and held as the natural fundamental values of human and social existence. Critical individualism, freedom, the equality of all men, the universality of law, toleration and the right to private property: these are what may be called the common denominator of the thought of the Enlightenment, a common denominator challenged only at one or two points, for example the right to private property, by the members of the extreme wing of the movement like Morelly and Mably. It is on the basis of these fundamental values which they held in common that the thinkers of the Enlightenment proceeded in their individually different ways to construct their concept of the world.

The scientific part of this concept had already been developed in the seventeenth century by Galileo, Descartes and Newton, and the French Enlightenment of the eighteenth century was generally content to adopt their results. Although this is a digression from the subject, it is worth mentioning that the development of modern natural science is one of the great successes to be credited to rationalist and empiricist thought. The idea that nature is a book written in mathematical language, that the entire universe is governed by general laws that know no exception; the elimination of all that is mysterious or strange or unusual, and the virtual elimination (although many scientists cautiously refrained from making this part of their theory explicit) of the miraculous; the assumption of constant, unchanging natural laws conforming to reason (Malebranche, who was a priest as well as a philosopher, held that God worked only through general laws); the assertion that these laws require confirmation by experience: these were the scientific advances of the seventeenth century inherited by the age of the Enlightenment.

Consequently, while there were several important scientists among the thinkers of the eighteenth century, especially Buffon and d'Alembert, the French Enlightenment was primarily concerned with questions of moral philosophy, religion and politics. Its task was to find answers to these questions in terms of the values listed above.

First the moral question. Once the adult and completely independent status of individual reason has been proclaimed and all trans-individual authority rejected, the problem is to establish a set of binding rules of conduct based only on the recognition of their validity by the individual conscience. The problem has remained unsolved to this day, though the progress of historical development has made it ever more urgent. To give it its modern name, it is the problem of *nihilism*.

Traditional Christian thought based the rules governing human conduct on the will of God, or (in the semi-rationalized form of this view) on natural reason, which God has implanted in the human soul.

The leading philosophers of the dialectical school, Hegel, Marx, Lukács and Heidegger, however much they differ on other questions, hold in common the fundamental view that man is an active part of the Whole (totality or being). Thus human values are part of existing reality, and are derived from it; at the same time reality itself becomes a value and a criterion of value.

Between the age of traditional Christianity and the beginning of dialectical philosophy there grew up the great individualist traditions which have continued to develop to this day: rationalism, empiricism and the Enlightenment. These traditions dispensed with all trans-individual concepts of God, community, totality and being. In doing so, they completely separated the two forms of individual consciousness, knowledge of facts and judgement of values. Science had become 'morally neutral' in the seventeenth century, and the problem of the Enlightenment was to find some other objective basis for value-judgements. The individualist perspective allows only three possible answers:

(a) The denial that value-judgements or general rules can in any way be based on the individual conscience. This view is content to assert that if every individual rationally pursues his self-interest and greatest happiness, society will function satisfactorily of itself.

(b) The assertion that rules in conformity with the general good can be based on human reason, which is held to be identical in all people.

(c) The hypothesis that every individual's own pursuit of his own greatest satisfaction can provide the basis of a number of rules promoting the general good. These rules claim no universal validity, but at least they make practical agreement possible and ensure the satisfactory working of social institutions.

The difference between the first of these answers and the two others is that the first explicitly renounces the possibility of generally accepted trans-individual standards. The two others set themselves the impossible task of grounding such standards in the individual reason or the individual pursuit of the greatest satisfaction.

The first answer, the most radical one, was formulated in seventeenth-century France: by Descartes, in a brief passing comment, and much more definitely by the individualist poet, Corneille. It is the assertion that the divorce between knowledge and value-judgement removes all possibility of justifying any moral values as universally binding.

When Princess Elizabeth of the Palatinate asked for generally valid rules of conduct, Descartes' first answer ran:

There is another truth whose knowledge seems to me most useful. It is that, although each of us is a person distinct from all others, whose interests are consequently to some extent different from those of the rest of the world, we must

always remember that none of us could exist alone, and each one of us is in fact one of the many parts of the universe, and more particularly a part of the earth, the state, the society, and the family to which we belong by our domicile, our oath of allegiance, and our birth. And the interests of the whole, of which each of us is a part, must always be preferred to those of our individual personality.
(15 September 1645)

This rule, he added, should be obeyed 'with measure and discretion'.

The subtle princess replied that, without in any way doubting the validity of these rules, she could still not see exactly how to base them on Descartes' philosophy or bring them into harmony with the rest of his thought. This was a crucial question, and it forced Descartes to retreat. Three weeks later he sent her the following reply, which is strongly characteristic of his thought:

I grant that it is difficult to measure exactly the extent to which reason bids us devote ourselves to the public interest; but it is not a matter calling for great precision. It is enough to satisfy one's conscience, and in doing so one can still leave much room for one's own inclination. For God has so established the order of things, and so closely bound men together in society, that even if every man acted only in his own interest and had no fellow-feeling for others, he would still not cease in the ordinary way to be acting in their interests as much as in his own, provided that he was prudent, particularly if he was living in an age whose morals were not corrupted. (6 October 1645)

We have here a schema often repeated in the Enlightenment: the assertion that the private and the public interest coincide. The inference, generally not drawn explicitly but still implicit in the Enlightenment, and later one of the fundamental concepts of the classical economists, is that it suffices to act in one's own interest without paying any regard to the general interest.

Compared with Descartes, the men of the Enlightenment were too deeply committed to the struggle with the existing political order (and compared with the classical economists, they were not yet sufficiently detached from the struggle)—a struggle undertaken in the name of the general good—to allow a concept so important to them to disappear completely.

Apart from the exchange of letters quoted, Descartes was content with a provisional ethic and made no attempt to develop his promised definitive moral system based on his philosophical premises. The ethic of nobility (*générosité*) postulates only the autonomy of the will and implies no particular principle of conduct towards others.

In the same way France's greatest individualist poet, Corneille, after four celebrated plays with 'noble' heroes (*Le Cid*, *Horace*, *Cinna* and *Polyeucte*) suddenly found that the same dramatic structure was suitable when the hero was self-seeking and vicious. Before tackling the composition of such plays (e.g. *Attila*) he wrote two transitional dramas (*Rodogune* and *Héraclius*) whose chief characteristic is that virtue and vice are treated as morally equal.

The argument is not that the individualist view is incompatible with any moral system, but, on the contrary, that it is compatible with *all* moralities, and thus entirely neutral between them. This is precisely why, on the basis of individualism, no system of values can be established as necessarily valid.

This problem is more immediate than ever in modern western industrial society. In this society an immense growth of scientific knowledge has given men vast power over nature. But at the same time it becomes constantly more clear that this rational knowledge is morally neutral and can contribute nothing to the establishment of any moral position or any scale of values. As I have said, the impossibility of establishing the necessity of any values within the dominant rationalist world vision is the structural basis of nihilism.

It must be constantly stressed that the fundamental moral neutrality of the individualist approach refers only to values of *content*, to relations of love, hate or indifference to others. In contrast to these are the *formal* values already listed—freedom, equality, toleration—and the concept of justice, which, as will be seen, is closely linked with them. In history these are intimately bound up with individualism, and, so long as they can be realized *without difficulty*, still retain their dominant position in western capitalist society. But, just because individualism in the last resort is morally neutral, there is always the danger that in a serious crisis they may be displaced by the opposite values. National Socialism in Germany was the greatest and most frightening instance of this, but unfortunately not the only one.

The subject of this essay, however, is not present-day society but the individualist thought of the eighteenth century and the French Enlightenment. Its thinkers were engaged in a fierce struggle with religion, tyranny and despotism. It was thus important for them to show that the values actually accepted by the bourgeoisie of the time could best be derived, quite independently of religious authority, from individual reason. It is not surprising that the great thinkers of the period totally failed to perceive the difficulty of basing these generally accepted values on the individual conscience. The only exception—and he stands on the fringe of the Enlightenment—is the Marquis de Sade, who developed a fully rational and systematic attitude to the world based on scorn and hatred. On the radical wing of the movement writers like Mably and Morelly based their values on reason. Some of the Encyclopedists, for instance d'Holbach and Helvétius, asserted simply that moral laws come from the individual's pursuit of his own happiness, and that it is in his interest to promote the general welfare since his own happiness depends on other people. If, therefore, men are immoral, it is generally through ignorance and a mistaken view of their true interests.[1]

Helvétius, who incidentally is one of the founders of sociological thought, was clearer-sighted and understood that things are more complicated. He agreed with d'Holbach's view that

[1] This question is rather more complex, as will be seen below.

moral laws are to be derived from private interest. But he saw that private interests vary from one social group to another. He accordingly drew the distinction between society as a whole and social sub-groups. We may quote a chapter heading from his book *De l'Esprit* (Essay II, 'The Mind relatively to Society'):

> It is proposed to prove in this discourse that the same interest which influences the judgement we form of actions, and makes us consider them as virtuous, vicious, or allowable, according as they are useful, prejudicial, or indifferent with respect to the public, equally influences the judgement we form of ideas; and that, as well in subjects of morality as in those of genius, it is interest alone that dictates all our judgements; a truth that cannot be perceived in its full extent without considering probity and genius relatively, 1. to an individual, 2. to a small society, 3. to a nation, 4. to different ages and countries, and 5. to the whole world.

By inquiring into the relation between the interests of a social group and its dominant morality, Helvétius laid the foundations of social science. Had he pursued the inquiry to its furthest limits he would have transcended the thought of the Enlightenment and reached the philosophy of history. But he was too much a man of his time and was too much under the influence of the Enlightenment to go more than half way. He decided accordingly that there exists in every man, besides the system of thought and value-judgement produced by his education and suitable for his social group, the possibility of more objective judgement and valuation, which in the last resort allows him to put the general interests of mankind above those of his own group. On this basis he distinguishes between 'virtues of prejudice' and 'true virtues'. The former reflect the interests of particular groups, the latter look to the interests of all mankind. By this roundabout way we are brought back to d'Holbach's line of argument.

Diderot adopted the same basic principles, but, as he usually did, he had a clearer awareness of their limitations, and wavered between the various views, which seemed to him equally justifiable but irreconcilable. The more moderate thinkers of the Enlightenment, particularly the English philosophers and Rousseau, assumed an inborn sense of fellowship or love of others, which allowed them to build up society and morality from single individuals' pursuit of their own happiness, or at least allowed them to think this possible in particular circumstances.

Whatever view one adopts, the problem remains that of basing the dominant bourgeois morality on the individual conscience. It remains unsolved, but the men of the Enlightenment, absorbed in their struggle against religion and despotism, were generally never aware of the fact.

Their moral teaching, despite the diversity of their systems, contains many similar elements, for its content reflects the dominant moral concepts of the middle and upper bourgeoisie of the time.[1] But there is the important distinction that Rousseau and the radicals saw the division between the individual and the general interest, and based the values they adopted on 'reason' or 'nature', while d'Holbach and the Encyclopedists inclined to the view that the general good is in harmony with the interests of the individual.

Religion

Passing to the religious ideas of the Enlightenment, we must start by distinguishing two problems to be treated separately:

(a) the religious ideas of the *philosophes* derived from the writers' own mental categories;

(b) the relation between the Enlightenment and Christianity.

For all their differences on religious questions (needless to say, within a limited area of divergence), all the writers of

[1] The morality of the two groups has much in common; they diverge on a number of important points, e.g. on the question of pleasure and self-denial, and therefore on sexual morality in general. On the other hand they share the values of compassion, feeling for one's fellow men, respect for the human person and, subject to legal qualifications, respect for the rights of property.

the Enlightenment are united in their hostility to traditional Christianity and the Church.

For the moment, however, we are not concerned with this hostility, but with the examination of the philosophers' own religious views. At first glance there seem to be three fundamental concepts: the atheism of the leading Encyclopedists, Voltaire's deism, and the theism of Rousseau and Mably. It might be thought that theism and deism are merely trivially different forms— adopted as concessions to prevailing opinion—of a fundamentally atheist world vision. Traditional Christianity had often treated them in these terms, and this was the view taken by Pascal, Garasse and several other seventeenth-century apologists. Another suggestion that has been made with some reason is that deism and theism constitute the first ideological concessions by the bourgeoisie to their fear of the people. Religion, a superfluity in addressing an educated audience, could still be useful, perhaps even necessary, if the uneducated masses of the poor were to be kept in check.

But though the god of Voltaire and Rousseau may have little in common with the transcendent god of Christianity, and though the *philosophes* often admitted the need for a double standard of truth, depending on whether they were addressing the cultivated classes or the uneducated masses, it remains clear none the less that their religious thought has its origin in the structure of their philosophical conception of the world.

I have already said that all the leaders of the Enlightenment regarded the life of a society as a sort of sum, or product, of the thought and action of a large number of individuals, each of whom constitutes a free and independent point of departure. This view inevitably raises the question of how to obtain at least the minimum of agreement needed to make society as a whole function tolerably smoothly, if not perfectly. All the *philosophes*, however critical they were of the existing order of politics and society, were convinced that it was at least possible to base an ideal social order on freedom, equality and toleration.

They thought of the physical and the social world as a vast

machine, consisting of separate, independent parts more or less well put together. There was nothing strange about such a machine; it was merely a greatly enlarged version of the machines that had become common in their time and had so impressed the Encyclopedists.

The 'machine' however could function only if, like any other, it was built by a competent mechanic on a deliberately worked out plan. Hence the image of God as the great clock maker, the designer and builder of the universe, and its constant recurrence in the literature of the Enlightenment.

Thus the deist or theist god of the Enlightenment is no mere concession to tradition, no mere bogey to frighten the uneducated, but *an essential part of the inner theoretical structure* of any rationalist or even semi-rationalist vision of the world. (The empiricists were confronted by the same problem, but it was possible for them to dismiss it as insoluble without contradicting themselves.)

The question had already arisen in the seventeenth century, and even then the individualist philosophers, in considering the principle that holds the separate constituent parts of the universe together, had been obliged to place it outside the universe in the will of a transcendent god. Leibniz's pre-established harmony, Malebranche's sole efficient cause working solely through general laws, Spinoza's psycho-physical parallelism—these are answers to a problem that continued to occupy the philosophers of the eighteenth century, and in its popularized form it led to the image of the great clock maker. It is worth adding that in several of the philosophers of the Enlightenment this image is tinged with optimism. The great clock maker has constructed no ordinary machine, but one that is *wonderful*, one that makes it possible for people, if only they will be sensible, to lead contented, happy lives. This optimism is connected with the objective conditions in which the *philosophes* were conducting their struggle. Furthermore the same line of thought appears in the defenders of Christianity. This explains the amazing popularity of the physico-theological Argument from Design.

Politics

At first glance the political principles of the Enlightenment seem a simple matter: freedom, equality, general application of the law, rejection of arbitrary rule, toleration, regard for the common good. The general attitude is clear, even if there are differences. The radicals wanted economic as well as political equality, advocating, as did Morelly and Mably, the abolition of private ownership of land, or, following Rousseau, its limitation. The moderates, on the other hand, were interested only in equality before the law.

In fact the problem is more complicated. When the *philosophes* examined the political order as it was and asked what it should be, they found themselves faced with another contradiction whose origins lay at the very centre of their thought. The view of man adopted by individualist thought, particularly in the Enlightenment, is *static* and entirely lacks the historical dimension. It acknowledges only one form of society, the 'natural' one.[1] All political and social systems that depart from this pattern were considered corrupt in proportion to the extent of their divergence. The corruption seemed all the greater as the mechanistic conception of nature and society adopted by many of the *philosophes*, especially the Encyclopedists, led them to think of the human will as determined by the natural and social environment.

On the other hand the *philosophes* were fighting a social and political system which they more or less completely rejected as basically corrupt. They were accordingly obliged to face a series of questions to which their system of thought offered no easy solution. Whether they followed Rousseau and placed the state of nature at the beginning of history or considered it something inherent in man as a reasonable being, they could not escape the question how mankind had departed from this ideal condition and fallen into corruption. In general the *philosophes* had a simple answer: it was fear, they said, in the hearts of the earliest men,

[1] The importance attached in the eighteenth century to the concept of the 'natural' is well known. It lies behind the stereotype of the 'noble savage', which is among those that best exemplify the thought of the period.

that enabled tyrants and priests to destroy their freedom and keep them in ignorance, deceive them with prejudices and thus corrupt their morals. This state of things could be changed only by the removal of prejudice and the diffusion of knowledge. (Most of the *philosophes* were opposed to the idea of a revolt that would transform the nature of society, not only because they were themselves bourgeois, but also because the idea invoked a concept of *historical* reality that was alien and even hostile to the structure of their thought.)

It must be added that the social background to the optimism of the *philosophes* was the actual development of French society as it moved with increasing speed toward the Revolution. *How* history advanced was a question the *philosophes* could easily ignore or answer superficially, since at the time it was not a question of acute urgency for French society to resolve. By contrast the discovery of the systematic philosophy of history in German idealism (from Kant's writings on historical philosophy to the true philosophy of history in Hegel) was more than anything a reflection of the fact the German bourgeoisie was much too weak to transform society and adapt it to its own interests.

There was a second, much harder question. How was prejudice to be overcome if the corrupted thought of the time, itself determined by prejudice, was the inevitable product of a corrupt social situation which could be made healthy or abolished only by sane thought untainted by prejudice? At this point the thought of most of the *philosophes* fell into a vicious circle from which there was no easy escape. Generally they took refuge in the hope of a 'miracle', an 'educator', a 'law-giver', above all an enlightened, educated government founded on law, which would create the new social and political conditions needed for the advance of society. This was certainly a contradiction in their philosophy. How could the good teacher or legislator appear in times that were fundamentally bad? Had not the *philosophes* themselves repeatedly shown that men are corrupted by unlimited power? Social history helps to explain the contradiction. Enlightened monarchies, particularly in the less advanced states of Europe like

Prussia, Austria and Russia, were fulfilling a modern, progressive role which strongly favoured the development of the middle class against the resistance of outworn traditional forms of society.

This explains how the *philosophes*, who were paving the way to the French Revolution, came to support the absolute rulers of Central and Eastern Europe, building great hopes on Frederick II, Catherine the Great and even Maria Theresa. The close relations between Voltaire and Frederick, like those between Diderot and the Empress Catherine, are generally known. Later, of course, both Voltaire and Diderot were forced to admit that the actual policies of these monarchs, whom they had earlier idealized, hardly lived up to their expectations or their principles. But no other solution to the problem was possible while philosophical thought clung to individualism and did not advance to the historical dialectic. The 'alliance' of *philosophe* and despot became an established commonplace of history, despite Voltaire's subsequent breach with Frederick, and despite Diderot's late *Essay on the Reigns of Claudius and Nero*, a despairing defence of the Roman philosopher Seneca, who remained a Councillor at Nero's court and covered up the tyrant's misdeeds to the very day that the Emperor commanded him to commit suicide. Diderot's oftrepeated argument runs: Would it really have been better for Seneca to leave merely because he could have no prospect of destroying Nero's tyranny? If he stayed, there was still the hope of preventing some of his crimes.

Finally there is a fundamental contradiction in the social and political ideals of the Enlightenment which had important consequences both for the internal structure of the movement and for the future social and political development of Europe. This is the contradiction in a society based on private property, and thus, in the individualist view of the world, between two essential mental categories of the Enlightenment, freedom and equality. In such a society, either of these values, if fully accepted, entails a definite restriction on the other. Complete freedom, unlimited by certain essential restraints, is bound to produce extensive

36

economic and social—and therefore political—inequality. On the other hand an individualist society cannot establish social equality without sharply limiting the freedom to accumulate wealth or abolishing private ownership altogether.

Inner structure of the movement

That completes the general description of the fundamental categories of the Enlightenment and their internal relations. But in addition, the Enlightenment, like every ideological movement, had an inner structure in which various tendencies can be distinguished. It is regrettable that we are still far from possessing the knowledge needed for the structural and sociological analysis of these tendencies. But we can at least say that the structure of the movement as a whole takes its pattern from the internal contradictions in its thought described above.[1]

The first major grouping of the thinkers of the French Enlightenment comprises those who place the main emphasis on equality. This approach led them to take a pessimistic view of historical development and to adopt a sharply critical attitude to the existing individualist social order. They accordingly worked out a programme for an ideal society based on reason. The group includes the radical wing, Mably, Morelly and Meslier, who, to ensure the equality of all members of society, not only called for major restrictions on freedom, but also abandoned one of the other basic ideas of the Enlightenment, the private ownership of land, which they denounced as a great evil.

There is, it is true, a certain similarity between this view and that of modern socialism, but there are also fundamental differences. In the first place, the *philosophes* attempted no historical analysis of the kind that might have laid bare the true

[1] But it should be observed that these internal contradictions do not provide a sufficient explanation in themselves for the division of the movement into separate currents. The currents appear only when the contradictions become *consciously known to men*. Such conscious knowledge in its turn is based on *social* causes; in the case of the Enlightenment these have not yet, to the best of my knowledge, been analysed.

historical forces working towards their ideal; second, their attitude led them to base their social ideal on 'nature' or 'reason', so that fundamentally they are believers in 'spirit', while modern socialist thought is essentially materialist, and therefore closer to that of the less radical wing of the Enlightenment.

The great differences separating figures like Mably or Morelly from modern socialist thought can be made clear by the fact that Mably based his social ideal on the aristocratic constitution of Sparta and was sharply critical of the Periclean democracy of Athens, while Morelly, in his *Code de la nature*, proposed to ban all research and speculation on world visions and the nature of spirit, hoping by these means to establish government on his principles once and for all.

I said earlier in this essay that the *philosophes* had moved away from the rationalism of Descartes and tended to favour Locke's empirical approach. It would be more accurate to say that the radical thinkers mentioned above were those whose view of the world retained more elements of Cartesianism than any of the others. If dualism of perception and reason, and of body and soul, is one of these elements, then Rousseau belongs to the radical wing. Although he did not advocate the abolition of private property, he placed great emphasis on equality and was a severe critic of the inequalities in modern society. Unlike the radicals, however, Rousseau did not abandon the idea of freedom, on which he based his theory of the social contract, or the right to own property; but he too encounters the problem of the relation between private property, freedom and inequality, and is thus led to consider the possibility and necessity of preventing excessive private wealth. Rousseau's ideal seems to be a kind of *petit-bourgeois* democracy, whose members are both free and equal, and none *very* rich or *very* poor.

Rousseau thus stands half-way between the radical opponents of private property on the one side and the Encyclopedists and Voltaire on the other. Despite considerable differences, he had much in common with the radicals: the rejection of materialism, the ideal of a social order based on reason, a critical attitude to the process of historical development that had created inequality, and the desire to reduce the economic effect of this inequality; but he joins the other main current of the Enlightenment, that of Voltaire and the Encyclopedists, in accepting fundamental limitations to the ideal of equality in order to safeguard freedom.

The leading figures of the group formed by the Encyclopedists, Diderot, d'Holbach and also Helvétius (who belongs to them although he was not a contributor), are above all empiricists inclining towards materialist monism. Their great exemplar is not Descartes but Locke. They take a positive view of historical development, particularly of the technology of craftsmanship and industry. For obvious reasons it is among them that the extreme atheists are to be found—those thinkers whose *social* ideas were the most radical needed some authority on which to found their ideal society (as opposed to existing society), and consequently inclined to deism or even theism.

In considering the religious views of the Encyclopedists it is important to distinguish between the 'official' point of view adopted in the *Encyclopédie* and their real opinions, as expressed in their other writings. Intellectually the *Encyclopédie* was a powerful attack on the prejudice and ignorance of the *ancien régime*; but it was also a large-scale economic enterprise, requiring heavy investment and dependent on the support of highly placed officials sympathetic to progressive ideas and ready to protect the publication against the suspicions of the authorities. Thus it had to find a large enough body of subscribers and to count on escaping the censor's ban through the help of friends in the machinery of government. (The ban was twice imposed and twice withdrawn.) Both the support of subscribers and the toleration of the authorities were conditional on moderation of language. Hence numerous articles in the *Encyclopédie* emphatically affirm the truth of Christianity and the positive character of the French monarchy, particularly in its existing form. This in no way prevented informed readers from realizing that the true purpose of these articles was to call these assertions into question and encourage the opposite opinions. The device was not new. Bayle

D

had used it in his *Dictionnaire*, and the authorities were well acquainted with it, so that it could no longer be used so blatantly. Even so, together with the writings of d'Holbach, Rousseau and Helvétius (most of Diderot's critical works remained unknown during his lifetime), it is the *Encyclopédie* that did most to shake old habits of thought in the mass of the educated bourgeoisie and to construct the new mental categories pointing the way to the French Revolution.

Voltaire's philosophical opinions and his vision of the world were more moderate, but, perhaps for that very reason, more emphatic and polemical when they came into conflict with the reality of his time. Although he rejected the radical social ideas of Mably and Rousseau, as he did the materialist philosophy of Diderot, d'Holbach and Helvétius, and though he found it much easier than they to accept the enlightened despotism of Frederick the Great and often felt that his attitude was in harmony with his own; though he believed (as he wrote in *Le Mondain*) in paradise (transferring it from heaven to the Paris of his day), he was still, with his light, witty, pointed style, one of the fiercest of the fighters against religious intolerance and the Catholic Church in general. Voltaire's work represents perhaps only a small section of the total composite view of the Enlightenment; but it is an essential part of the struggle, and, both for its extent and for its excellence, of primary importance to this aspect of the movement.

The 'economists'—or, more exactly 'physiocrats'—belong to the most moderate part of the movement, associated with it less by the actual content of their opinions than by the mental categories from which those opinions derive. They defended 'despotism' (their name for absolute monarchy), but, in place of the old theory of Divine Right and respect for tradition and revelation, they developed a monarchical theory founded on the rationalist mental categories of the Enlightenment and shaped in terms of those same categories. They are of great importance in the history of the social sciences, not merely because they established political economy as an objective science, but also because in the 'Tableau Économique' they worked out the first *complete model* of the total economic process. The bourgeois classical economists, still working within the structure of fundamental individualism, could not have grasped the significance of this total process. The conceptual model regains its strength in Marx's *Capital*, in the work of the later Marxists and, since Schumpeter, in bourgeois academic economics.

The principal idea of the physiocrats was that, in a country where capital was chiefly invested in agriculture rather than industry, the removal of all restrictions on private wealth and the establishment of a fully free economy would produce a large enough national income to allow the existence of both a third estate, living on earned income and profit, and a strong land-owning class (they meant of course 'aristocracy'), living on continuously rising rents. The co-existence of a strong bourgeoisie and a strong nobility could then be made the basis of a modern enlightened monarchy. The physiocrats were naturally the *bête noire* of the radicals, especially Mably, who denounced their 'economism' in the name of 'spirit' and 'virtue'. This once again shows the difficulty of drawing any parallels between the radical wing of the Enlightenment and later socialist thought, and the care needed in handling the similarities as well as the differences in this area.

Criticism of bourgeois values

Rousseau The foregoing is an attempt to outline the general structure of the French Enlightenment. Naturally each of the *philosophes* gives his own version of the thought contained within this general structure; and although it is beyond the scope of this essay to consider them individually in detail, it should be noted that two of the outstanding thinkers of the movement, Rousseau and Diderot, in contrast to all the others, recognized and understood its negative aspects and inner contradictions. Rousseau emphasized those of bourgeois society, Diderot those of the Enlightenment itself. This explains why Kant, Goethe and Hegel, the leaders of the German idealist school which superseded the philosophy of the Enlightenment, rated their contributions the highest.

The ideal society conceived by many of the *philosophes*, particularly the group round d'Holbach and Helvétius, and by moderates like Voltaire, was an idealized form of existing bourgeois society. Some of them indeed, for example d'Holbach, pushed this 'socio-centrism' to the point where they could hardly see the possibility of divergence between private interest and public good. Rousseau however was sharply critical of a society built up on conflicting private interests. His two celebrated tracts, the *Discours sur les sciences et les arts* and the *Discours sur l'origine et les fondements de l'inégalité parmi les hommes*, use arguments that turn precisely on the contrast of the non-antagonistic life of men living in a state of nature independently of each other (or the first communities of shepherds) with that of modern society, constructed as it is on rivalry, antagonism, boundless egoism and *amour propre*. This established the fundamental concept of his world vision—that in terms of human morality the development of society is not progress but its reverse. Voltaire and other *philosophes* do not seem justified in criticizing him for wanting to restore society to its primitive state; Rousseau knew well enough that this was impossible. But in seeking an alternative to this negative evolution he did not choose the kind of historical analysis that could have shown him the forces working against social deterioration and capable perhaps of changing its course to a progressive direction. Instead, in his *Social Contract* he depicts an ideal society based on the essential categories of the Enlightenment—freedom, equality, toleration and contract; he believed it possible to realize such a society through the moral forces inherent in men and capable of development under the influence of a good government and a good educator. At this point he meets the same difficulty as all the other *philosophes*: since society has fallen from grace and become corrupt, he cannot say where good legislation and a good educator are to be found. But it is to his credit that his fundamentally democratic convictions made him prefer to leave the question unanswered rather than follow Voltaire and Diderot in acclaiming a Frederick the Great or an Empress Catherine and hoping to find a solution in despots of their sort.

It is also important to note the significance of Rousseau's abstract and purely schematic distinction between the 'bad', purely self-seeking member of existing society and the 'good' citizen participating in the general will and ready to place himself in total submission to a society constructed on the social contract. This distinction enabled Rousseau to see more clearly than the other *philosophes* the division of the individual in bourgeois society into the concrete self-centred private person on the one hand, and the abstract 'citoyen' serving the general interest on the other. This division is a basic characteristic of modern man. But Rousseau developed the distinction within the framework of the categories of the Enlightenment; he was able to make an abstract contrast between the two roles of the individual, but he did not understand that they act upon each other and really form two parts—simultaneously complementary and contradictory—of a single concrete totality.

It is only in German idealism, starting with Kant, that Rousseau's analysis of the relation between private man and 'citizen', selfish interest and the general good, 'vice' and 'virtue', is first transcended. Though Kant maintains the abstract form of the distinction, he no longer treats it as the expression of two different forms of society, the real and the ideal, but as a contradiction in the individual conscience of every man between the demands of self-gratification and morality. The fact that both philosophers based their thought on this abstract distinction is probably one of the main reasons for Kant's high opinion of Rousseau.

It remained for dialectical thought to find the real analysis of the relations between bourgeois society and the state, the private man and the 'citoyen', and to see that these were merely different but mutually conditioned aspects of a particular form of social organization.

Diderot Diderot seems to me to occupy as important a position as Rousseau—perhaps a more important one—in the history of western thought. In the first place, he resolutely defended the values of the Enlightenment one by one against those who actually opposed the bourgeoisie socially and politically, and against theoretical critics. But in addition to this, both in some of his minor published works and in some major writings that he himself did not publish, he set about questioning the value not only of bourgeois society and its ideology but also of many of the fundamental categories of the Enlightenment itself. This made it possible for him to be simultaneously the organizer and guiding spirit of the *Encyclopédie*, with which his name is so closely linked that one can hardly think of them apart, and one of the greatest essayists in the intellectual history of western Europe.

There is of course a definite relation between the *Encyclopédie* and the essay form; otherwise a figure like Diderot would be unthinkable. But there is more fundamentally a decisive contradiction within the relation. It would be almost impossible to imagine an essay by d'Holbach or Helvétius, while Diderot is above all one of the three or four great essayists in literary history. How can we explain the difference?

The *Encyclopédie* belongs to the quintessential nature of the Enlightenment. The essay first appears at the beginning of the rise of individualist thought in that incomparable model for all essayists, Michel de Montaigne, *grand seigneur* and member of the *Parlement*, who questioned all the values of the traditional world vision. At the end of the period, when the first steps were being taken forward from the Enlightenment towards dialectical thought, the outstanding essayist is the amiable Denis Diderot, son of a small-scale knife manufacturer, who gave the bourgeois world vision its most remarkable expression in the *Encyclopédie*, and then began to doubt and question that vision himself.

The great difference between the *Encyclopédie* and the essay is like that between the knowledge which answers questions and the kind of question to which at the time there is no knowledge capable of giving an answer. The *Encyclopédie* is above all a collective enterprise which undertook to make the sum of existing knowledge available to the public and to future generations. The Encyclopedists of course realized that this knowledge constituted only a small part of what generations to come would add to the amount hitherto amassed. The progress of knowledge knows no limits. Wagner's remark in *Faust*, 'Much though I know, I would know all', is only a parody (though not a completely unfair one) of the Encyclopedists' motto, which could be more exactly put as: 'Though I know something, I would know far more, and advance as far as possible along a road on which our successors will far outstrip us.' The true form of the rationalist concept of knowledge is the image, well known in the Middle Ages and often recalled later, of dwarfs riding on a giant's back and, small as they are, able to see farther than the giant himself. None the less the Encyclopedists considered the fundamental categories listed earlier in this essay as definitive achievements of the human mind; and it was these categories—the individual consciousness as the arbiter of truth, the generality of all laws, the natural freedom and equality of all men, human nature as the basis of private property —that Diderot questioned.

A word is needed on the literary classification of the essay. If an essay were not more than a theoretical examination of particular truths, it would cease to be a literary form of its own kind and would be classified as a type of philosophical treatise. The opponents of scepticism had long since shown that radically sceptical thought is self-contradictory, since, if it is to be consistent, it can make no claim to be true; if you say that nothing is true, you cannot claim truth for that statement either.

But though the inspiration is generally sceptical, its point of departure lies in an attitude far removed from scepticism. What matters to the essayist is not the actual process of examining the theoretical basis of particular truths or values. Instead he is concerned with showing that such an examination is both possible and necessary, and, at the same time, that it is both important and yet impossible to give answers. He is looking for theoretical answers to a series of questions fundamental to human existence which can have no prospect of ever being answered from his point of view.

That gives the essay form its originality. Literary works are complex worlds of their own, created and constructed by the writer's imagination out of particular people and things and concrete situations; philosophical works are abstract and conceptual expressions of particular world visions. The essay is both abstract and concrete. Its nature, like that of philosophy, is chiefly to raise certain conceptual questions fundamental to human life; but, unlike most philosophy, it has neither the desire nor the ability to answer them. Like literature, it puts these questions not in a conceptual form but attaches them to the 'occasion' of a concrete person or situation taken both from literature and (as the greatest essayists do) from real life. The true essay thus necessarily inhabits two worlds, and is necessarily ironic: it seems to be talking about particular people and situations, but these are mere 'occasions' for the esssayist to raise crucial abstract questions. In this way it is Diderot's habit to use concrete situations as 'occasions' for questions that treat the thought of the Enlightenment as a problem in itself.

His best-known essay, *Le Neveu de Rameau*, is one of those he did not publish. After his death it was discovered by Goethe, who issued it in a German translation. It was then used by Hegel in the *Phenomenology* as one of the figures of Mind.

The philosopher encounters the great composer's nephew in a café. He cuts a curious figure, a tall, gaunt parasite living on the rich bourgeois whom he despises. He judges society and his own position completely without hypocrisy, and by doing so in the light of his own experience he calls into question all the apparently established truths of bourgeois society. During the conversation it becomes increasingly difficult to know which of the men is right: the philosopher, whose defence of the 'general principles' of the bourgeois order and its morality becomes increasingly half-hearted, or the sponger, using his actual experience of this order and its morality to show what they really look like in a particular case and to demonstrate the inadequacy, and often the complete falsity, of seemingly unshakeable truths.

It will be best to use Hegel's own words to show the limits of the thought of the Enlightenment and the manner in which it is transcended.

On the one side we have

> the content uttered by spirit and uttered about itself. . . .
> This style of speech is the madness of the musician 'who piled and mixed up together some thirty airs, Italian, French, tragic, comic, of all sorts and kinds' . . . the inversion and perversion of all conceptions and realities, a universal deception of itself and others. The shamelessness manifested in stating this deceit is just on that account the greatest truth.

The philosopher on the other hand is

> a placid soul that in simple honesty of heart takes the music of the good and true to consist in harmony of sound and uniformity of tone . . . regards this style of expression as a 'fickle fantasy of wisdom and folly, a mêlée of so much skill and low cunning, composed of ideas as likely to be right as wrong'.

But this talk of 'simple placid consciousness of the good and the true' is inevitably 'monosyllabic' in comparison with the other view, 'for it can say nothing to the latter that the latter does not know and say. . . . Its very syllables "disgraceful", "base", are this folly already', the folly of thinking one is saying something different or new to an interlocutor who 'already says it of himself'.

As to the answer that 'the good must not lose value because it may be linked with what is bad or mingled with it, for to be thus associated with badness is its condition and necessity, and the wisdom of nature lies in this fact'—this is no decisive answer but only a trifling summary of the other's assertion that 'the so-called noble and good is by its very nature the reverse of itself, or what is bad is, conversely, something excellent'. Nor can this argument be answered by proving 'the *reality* of what is excellent, when it produces an example of what is excellent, whether in the form of a fictitious case or a true story, and thus shows it not to be an empty name'. For in being forced to rely on an example the philosopher admits that this reality is exceptional, 'constitutes merely something quite isolated and particular, merely an "*espèce*", a *sort* of thing. And to represent the existence of the good and noble as an isolated particular anecdote, whether fictitious or true, is the bitterest thing that can be said about it.' Hegel then shows that, in writing this essay, Diderot moved beyond the view which he was purporting to represent.

In other essays, for instance in the *Entretien d'un père avec ses enfants*, Diderot uses the 'occasion' of particular concrete cases to raise questions like the following: If a general law is recognized as necessary and justified in itself, must it be obeyed here and now in every particular instance? Might not such obedience produce great injustice? The law must be general. For example, it is right that husband and wife must not inherit each other's property, for this prohibition is the only way to ensure harmony in marriage. But if a man has spent his entire fortune to care for his sick wife, and after her death finds money that belonged to her about which no one else knows, must he then obey the law and give it to her rich relatives and live in poverty himself? Or has he the right to appropriate the sum and thus compensate himself in part for the fortune he has given away? Diderot adduces similar cases but offers no answer. In *Les deux Amis de Bourbonne* he shows us two men who have come into conflict with the law. Their conduct towards each other is inspired entirely by altruism and love, and they are men of the noblest character, but society condemns them as worthless criminals.

Diderot's most comprehensive essay, *Jacques le fataliste*, consists of a long conversation between the fatalistic servant Jacques and his master. They exchange long accounts of their adventures, and we are constantly made to see how reality contrasts with common sense and prudence, how the servant is often really the master, and the master is dependent on the servant.

Diderot was the only *philosophe* to understand that, while men's behaviour may be determined by their social circumstances, these circumstances themselves result from the actions of men.

Although he came no nearer than Rousseau did to sketching even the outline of a dialectical philosophy (we do not find the elements of it before Kant), he was more aware than any of the other *philosophes* how complex the social world is; and it was with justice that not only Lessing but also Hegel and Goethe considered him one of the outstanding figures of the Enlightenment of the eighteenth century.

11 *The Enlightenment and Christian Belief*

It is both easy and difficult to speak of the relation between the Enlightenment and Christianity. The task is comparatively simple because for the socio-phenomenological analysis we have Groethuysen's excellent *Entstehung der bürgerlichen Welt- und Lebensanschauung in Frankreich*. Although this was intended as no more than the prolegomenon to a work that was left unfinished at the author's death, it carried the analysis of the conflict to an advanced point. The difficulty comes from the fact that it is not easy to fix the position of the Enlightenment in the development of the individualist world vision in terms of social history.

In my study of Pascal I wrote that there are three important stages in the history of French rationalism and that each of them assigned a qualitatively different place to the practical application of theory. I suggested that these stages are characterized by the terms in which each of them conceived the relation between rational thought and action.

To Descartes this was no problem at all: rational thought, in his view, automatically entails correct action, and the philosopher need concern himself only with the problem of the proper use of his reason.

Valéry, writing during one of the gravest crises of bourgeois society, found the connection between reason and action a major, insoluble problem. For him reason occupies a position of supreme importance, but possesses purely intellectual power and has almost no influence on the outside world, which the thinker can master in its sensible appearances only through poetry.

The Enlightenment stands between these stages of rationalism. It is characterized by its view of reason as *the* decisive weapon in the practical struggle against despotism, superstition, privilege, *ancien régime* and Christianity. This is what makes it necessary to see it in at least two perspectives in determining its position in the development of western thought.

On the one hand, rationalism and empiricism, the two principal forms of individualism, present a purely static world vision which knows nothing at all of the concept of historical becoming. Thus if we follow Hegel, Goethe and Marx in treating history and historical action as the only genuine content for human consciousness, we may truly say that the individualist world visions of the Enlightenment were purely formal and possessed no true content, as this historical consciousness ultimately remained alien to the movement. But if instead we take into account the fact that the struggle against the old social and political order, with its obsolete privileges, and likewise the battle with the Church, constituted real historic and progressive action, then the individualist view of the Enlightenment does, despite all its limitations, have a content, even if the movement never attained a dialectical awareness of its nature.

It would be more precise, and would take into account the fact that the individualist world vision remains alive in our own times, if we adopted a formula along the following lines: The individualist view possesses content only in certain historical situations; it did so most notably in the eighteenth century, but it can still do so now, whenever its basic values (freedom, equality, toleration, etc.) are in danger and need to be defended; however, when these values are dominant in society and not directly faced with any serious threat, individualism tends to revert to its purely formal character and lose the power of giving meaning to human life.

We have examples of both situations in the world today: in socialist countries, where the individualist values are in danger, and in western society, where they more and more appear formal and devoid of content.

In analysing the conflict with the Church we must always remember that the attacks the Enlightenment was making on Christian belief were not attacks on the faith of the pre-bourgeois period, the faith that built cathedrals and preached the crusades. The *philosophes* were battling against a faith whose content had been taken from it by the very social and economic processes that had promoted the growth of individualism; this faith had accordingly acquired much the same structural character as the Enlightenment itself. Had it been carried to its logical conclusion, this attenuated faith would have ended in theism, deism, or even atheism; but, just because it was not thought out logically, it turned into superstition and bigotry. As Hegel saw, this fact provides the historical justification for the critical attacks on religion made by the Enlightenment. But it must not be forgotten that Christian belief, however weakened, entailed some content in human thought and action even in the eighteenth century, and continued to assert that such a content was necessary. It was this requirement which led the German idealist and dialectical philosophers to undertake the major task of discovering a valid and authentic system to replace individualism. I shall return to this point in the last section of this essay, where I shall consider to what extent the effort met with success.

Earlier in this study I sketched the main features of Hegel's analysis in the *Phenomenology*, and that alone will have shown the difficulty of fixing the place of the Enlightenment in the history of ideas. It is possible (and in some ways justified) to see the movement as a stage in the development of the unhistorical individualist world vision; but it is equally justifiable to regard it, in its deliberate struggle against *ancien régime*, privilege and Church, as the beginning of man's awareness of himself as an active participant in the construction of human society and in its transformation through liberation from all transcendental authority.

At the same time it is possible to trace a line of thought, running from Descartes by way of Voltaire and perhaps also d'Holbach to Valéry, which contrasts the attitudes of these thinkers with the tragic vision of Pascal and the dialectic systems of Kant and Hegel. There is yet another approach that sees in Descartes, Voltaire and Diderot the beginning of modern non-transcendental thought and traces its development through German idealism and Marxism.

Christianity and the rationalized society

The work of Groethuysen mentioned above, though only the first section of it was completed, is an outstanding socio-historical study of the relation between the Enlightenment and the Christianity of the period. This book is all the more relevant to the subject of this essay because, unlike other synthesizing studies of the opposition between rationalism and religion (Paul Hazard's, for example), it does not confine itself to description of the anti-Christian polemics of the Enlightenment, the so-called 'trial of God'. Groethuysen probably intended to cover this area in the later sections of his work. At all events he concentrates on using contemporary sermons and other apologetic literature to reveal the newly established general mental structures of bourgeois thought. In this way he shows how these structures influenced not merely the attacks on Christianity but also the thought and writing of its defenders. As a result—with the single exception of the Jansenists, who rejected the modern world of their day, together with all the mental structures associated with it and reflecting it, and held fast to the Augustinian tradition— the dialogue between Christianity and the Enlightenment was conducted for the most part on common ground, that is to say, it assumed the mental categories of the Enlightenment. The acceptance of these in itself decided the outcome of the struggle in advance.

The traditional Christian belief of earlier centuries had developed in a society whose institutions were barely rationalized, if at all. This society was based on *qualitative* relations in which Christian faith played an essential and decisive part in determining the place of men in their social and natural environment.

In the eighteenth century on the other hand the dialogue between Christianity and the Enlightenment was conducted in a historical situation in which the most important social group, the middle class, had succeeded in rationalizing a large part of its life and organizing it on an intelligible pattern. In this world the citizen no longer regarded his social position as the outcome of divine grace or punishment, but as the result of his own conduct; whether his actions were appropriate and successful or misdirected and profitless, they were, at least in economic terms, morally neutral and incapable of being judged by standards of good and evil. In the Middle Ages it was possible to talk in terms of 'just' or 'unjust' prices; in the eighteenth century there were only correctly or mistakenly calculated prices. The right price was the one that fixed the difference between cost and selling price in such a way as to maximize profit; the wrong one was any that failed to secure the maximum gain.

With the development of the bourgeoisie this rationalized form of conduct occupied an ever more important place in society, and the argument between faith and reason was conducted in radically different terms from those used in the thirteenth century or even at the end of the Middle Ages. At that earlier time the problem was to take account of the newly developing towns and assign a place to rational thought and action in the totality of a life built on faith. By the eighteenth century the area of bourgeois life occupied by rational thought and action had grown so far that the *nature* of the question had altered. It was no longer a question of the place to be assigned to reason in a life built on faith, but rather of what place there could be for faith within a world vision grounded on reason. It was a question of what meaning the Christian god and Christianity in general could have in the eyes of the middle-class citizen, and of how faith could be made compatible with his everyday existence. This was the new social and intellectual background to the Enlightenment's campaign against religion, a campaign that Hazard aptly called 'the trial of God'. Needless to say the defenders of Christianity had to take this situation into account and, on the whole, accept it as a reality which the argument could not ignore.

One of Diderot's philosophical fragments (*Pensées philosophiques*, XVI) reads: 'A man was asked once if there were any real atheists. His reply was, "Do you believe there are any real Christians?"'

Whatever one's personal beliefs, it is essential, if one is to understand either the eighteenth century or modern society, to recognize that these words of Diderot's are no mere epigram but a crucial analysis whose content of truth has constantly been increased by the subsequent development of western society. It asserts that the development of the bourgeoisie has for the first time in history produced not merely a class that has generally lost its faith, but rather one whose practice and whose thought, whatever its formal religious belief, are *fundamentally* irreligious in a critical area, and totally alien to the category of the sacred.

Pascal, who opposed this development, defined human life, in a celebrated fragment, as an inescapable bet on the existence or non-existence of God. He meant that every human action is determined in its inmost structure by the fact that it either reckons divine intervention among its possible consequences or no longer regards divine intervention as a possibility at all.

In the thinking of people in earlier societies (a way of thought which persisted in the attitudes of peasants and labourers, the 'common people' of the eighteenth century), this possibility of divine intervention—as providential help here below, punishment or reward in the hereafter, or merely God's approval or wrath—was a factor in every human action and every common event. It thus constituted the psychological base of traditional belief.

In the eighteenth century, the newly developing economic area of bourgeois life is marked by the fact that probably for the first time in history an important part of the activity of a class growing in social importance has become a wager, in Pascal's sense, on the non-existence of God. The economic life of the bourgeoisie was in fact—or at least in its tendency—autonomous and morally neutral, governed only by the internal criteria of success or failure, and independent of the moral criteria of 'good' or 'wicked' and the religious criteria of 'pleasing to God' or 'sinful'.[1]

As the socio-historical process is one of extreme complexity, it would be entirely wrong to see this development as one in which the entire bourgeoisie lost its faith and took up arms against an unchanged system of Christian belief.

For one thing, as I have already said, Christianity itself was modified by this social and intellectual process; for another, only a small part of the bourgeoisie found the means of expressing the new world vision in a logically consistent form; and it did so only in the short period before a new social danger appeared in the popular rising of the French Revolution. By then the bourgeoisie had achieved its social and political aims, and it began to find religion useful as a 'social bulwark'.

Thus the sociological foundation of the Enlightenment is a social process which favoured the growth of anti-Christian mental structures and simultaneously entailed a structural alteration of Christian belief within its old external forms. This transformation characterizes not only the eighteenth century but, even more strikingly, western society in our own day.

To make the picture clearer, it will perhaps be useful to bring out some of the leading traits of the process, which have continued to develop, though sometimes in a different form, in the modern world.

The first crucial change in Christian belief was one that Groethuysen calls 'simultaneous loss of intensity and scope'. The notion of divine intervention was excluded from a major area of the life of the bourgeoisie and its picture of the world. It was

---

[1] It was also sometimes the case that the new bourgeois view of the world in particular circumstances created a corresponding religious form. Max Weber showed in a celebrated study the close links between protestant ethics and capitalism, placing, in my view, too much of the causative emphasis on the side of ethics. Protestantism was an authentic and concrete form of the historical development of the bourgeoisie, but it in no way diminished the emphasis placed in protestant countries, as well as catholic ones, on success as the guiding principle of economic life, though it did attach a religious meaning to success. In its later development, economic life gave up its religious form.

excluded not only from its economic life but also from its concept of the universe as ruled by general and unchangeable laws of nature. Many people excluded it also from their idea of the social mechanism, which they began to conceive, to some extent, in the same terms as the processes of nature. This exclusion caused many customs and traditions, together with the mental concepts underlying them, to lose all valid meaning in the new picture of the universe. These were the traditions and customs derived from the possibility of divine intervention in everyday life; but they did not disappear from the lives of peasants and labourers, and so came to look like ignorant superstition and to be contrasted unfavourably with the 'purified and spiritualized' religion of the bourgeoisie. This gave rise to the division of mankind into 'ignorant masses' and 'the educated classes' (meaning of course the bourgeois 'gentry'). This division is one of the most characteristic features of the Enlightenment.

The very fact that even the restricted form of religion was excluded from a growing area of everyday life caused it also to lose intensity. It became a sort of 'statement of principles', still capable of influencing family life and some other social relations, but unable to have any effect on the most important activities of the individual. Thus the 'loss of scope' brought with it a fundamental change in the character and content of religion. Groethuysen observes in this context that, while the act of professing Christianity had never involved a clear and conscious acceptance of all its articles of faith, the explicitly stated creed had in the past stood for a much larger implied content of belief. But if in earlier times there was no difficulty in regarding the profession of faith as including the wider acceptance, this became a problem in the eighteenth century. Feeling oneself a Christian no longer entailed acceptance of all the dogmas established and recognized by the Church; membership of the Church committed one only to those affirmations and articles of faith that one explicitly recognized oneself.

Previously unbelief had been an individual state and faith collective. Once scepticism had become a social phenomenon, faith tended to become an individual matter. It was no longer a case of 'we believe' but of 'I believe'; and it was the 'I' of the educated bourgeois that called for a spiritualized and rational religion.

At all events this development created a division between the religious and the secular domains of life. Daily life had earlier been permeated with religious images and mental structures; there now developed an economic life whose most prominent characteristic is its secular, 'deconsecrated' nature. Economic activity does more than occupy a large area of everyday bourgeois life; it extends over its own boundaries to influence numerous other everyday activities. Correspondingly the religious domain becomes a special and limited sector of individual life.

The close interpenetration of faith and daily life increasingly strikes the bourgeois as superstitious ignorance. His attitude corresponded to the reality of the newly developed social order, but its effect was to make the earlier tradition of weaving the hope of divine help and the fear of divine punishment into the fabric of daily life incomprehensible.

This is probably one of the most important features of the historical change. To this day it has remained impossible to give an affirmative reply to Diderot's question whether there exists a real Christian. That is because it asks whether bourgeois society can allow the existence of a man whose ordinary professional and economic life is Christian and not basically secular.

It is enough to consider the activity of a businessman or manufacturer to know what the answer must be. Such a man may of course live modestly, he may even practise self-denial and give all his profits to the poor or to the Church; what he cannot do is to earn his living in a 'Christian' or a 'sinful' way, 'morally' or 'immorally'. Economic life is secular, and therefore as totally alien to the categories of 'right' and 'wrong' as to 'Christian' and 'unchristian'.[1] Its only essential categories are those of success

---

[1] To state the point more clearly: in a society based on market production, economic activity can no more be 'moral' or 'immoral', 'Christian' or 'sinful', than an odour can be square or round, or a colour sweet-scented or evil-smelling.

and failure. It may perhaps give temporary acknowledgement to values recognized or condemned by the custom of the time, but it throws these overboard at the first sign of conflict between them and economic advantage.

This justifies Groethuysen's assertion that the tendency of the bourgeois is to take his faith 'in bulk' and to acknowledge its precise particular requirements less and less as binding. At the same time he no longer thinks of the Church as his community, or of his priest as an intermediary standing between himself and God. Church and priest become an organization to defend religious belief. It addresses itself to the judgement of the bourgeois, who can choose to join it if he accepts its claims as true, or perhaps merely thinks that his membership is generally to the advantage of society; and can join it without necessarily accepting every item of its doctrine.

But there is one central point on which the rational bourgeois is totally unable to accept Christian faith—the doctrine of original sin. This doctrine is based on a non-rational view of human life and society. But the life of the bourgeois is very largely rationalized; he does not think of himself as a saint or a sinner, but as a man, some of whose actions may be pleasing to God, and others sinful. As Groethuysen says in one of his chapter headings, the notion of 'sinner' is replaced by that of 'sin'.

As a result, the man of the Enlightenment judges the Christian god on the basis of his general mental categories of equality, freedom and moral respect for the basic human rights. This god is judged as one who allows only a few chosen souls to be sharers in Grace and delivers the rest to perpetual damnation; who is omnipotent but has created a world in which not all men can be happy and virtuous; who (in the Augustinian view) has simply denied to most men the freedom to abstain from sin; who is supposed to be the God of love but refuses forgiveness to the sins of countless millions. Naturally enough such a god came to seem a tyrant of the kind that only the basest superstition could have invented, one that could have nothing whatever in common with the true god of an enlightened, spiritualized religion.

The controversy over the nature of God well illustrates the close link between the thought of the Jesuits and their allies, who had adapted their views to the new society, and the anti-Christian thought of the Enlightenment. While the Jansenists defended the Augustinian tradition of God as an all-powerful figure beyond all human understanding, with whom man's only relation must be one of total submission and dependence, the Jesuits replied that this view ascribed a tyrannical nature to God which was repugnant to reason; and this is the very objection that the eighteenth-century *philosophes* raised against the entire notion of the Christian god. Two extracts from the immense literature of the time will be enough to illustrate the point. The first come from Groethuysen (op. cit., vol. 1, pp. 142–3), quoting a Jesuit sermon against the Jansenist image of God:

This is a God who is neither holy nor just nor merciful. . . .
He is nothing less than a merciless and barbarous tyrant
who deserves all my hatred, and yet this is the God whom
the Jansenists, with great emphasis on the commandment,
tell us we must love. . . . But how can we love their God,
how can I love God at all, if Quesnel depicts him in the
form that is most hideously distorted and best calculated to
make him hateful to me; After all this fine talk it turns out
that this God, to love whom is the sole virtue, this God
whom Quesnel forbids men to fear, is, in the eyes of this
same Quesnel, a tyrant who gives impossible commands, and
not content with that, adds to it the greater mercilessness of
condemning all who have not carried them out. Let us be
honest for once. Is this a God whom it is possible to love?

We find much the same idea in Diderot's early *Pensées
philosophiques*, written at a time when he was still a sceptical deist:

What voices! What cries! What groans! Who has enclosed
these piteous corpses in this dungeon? What crimes have all
these wretched ones committed? Some beat their breasts with
stones, some tear their bodies with nails of iron. The eyes of

all are filled with remorse, sorrow and death. Who condemns them to these torments? The God whom they have offended. . . . But what kind of God is this? Could a God of goodness take delight in bathing himself in these tears? Are not these terrors an offence to his mercy? If these were criminals assuaging a tyrant's wrath, what more could they do? (VII)

Presented with the picture that is painted of the Supreme Being, his swiftness to anger, the harshness of his vengeance, the proportion of those he leaves to perish to those to whom he deigns to stretch out his hand, the most upright soul might be tempted to wish that he did not exist. We could be calm enough in this world if we could be certain there was nothing to fear in the next. No one was ever frightened by the thought that there is no God; terror comes from the thought that there may be one, a God of the kind that is depicted. (IX)

For the same reasons the great decisive argument of the Church, the argument of death, which modern existentialism has revived in its secular form, loses its importance for the bourgeois. He has replaced the traditional conception of God with a radically different one, that of the 'good and just clock maker' who has constructed the wonderful machine of the universe, who loves all men alike, gives them freedom to sin or to avoid sin, and will punish them only for ingrained, unrepented sins. A man whose life has not been wicked beyond measure, and who repents his misdeeds, need no longer fear death as something terrible.

This view makes the fear of death appear more and more as individual cowardice, while those who have completely given up Christianity come to consider a calm and fearless death the worthiest of all ends to a serious and courageous life. The bourgeois who remains a Christian makes it his aim to set his relations with God in order by a 'Christian death', repenting his sins and receiving the last sacraments, much as he would settle his accounts and draw up his will.

A short digression is necessary at this point. It would be a mistake to assume a direct connection between individualism and the disappearance of the fear of death or, conversely, to see the reappearance of this fear as a return to traditional pre-individualist Christianity. While individualism remained the ideology of a rising social class, general anxiety, and particularly the fear of death, occupied only a small and secondary place, if any at all, in the thought of the bourgeois ideologists. In the great crisis of individualist society embracing roughly the period between 1914 and 1945, about which I shall have more to say, belief in the rational and intelligible ordering of the world and human society was shattered, and the problem of death acquired an ever-growing fundamental importance. Both socially and in terms of individual experience, the problem became something quite different from the fear of death in the Christian Middle Ages or earlier periods. Then death had been treated as a moment of supreme importance for the individual soul within an all-embracing totality of salvation. In the 'crisis of individualist society' the individual is seen, as he was in the eighteenth century, as the starting-point; but men's individual lives and actions have become a problem to them, and the values on which they are based have been called into question and require justification. Then death, seen not merely as the end of the individual life but also as the destruction of values, which have been built *entirely* on the life of the individual, suddenly becomes a terrifying, inescapable reality. This creates a subjective form of the individualist view of life, based on 'dereliction', 'dread' and 'decision', whose Christian and atheist forms are ultimately much closer to each other than either is to the Christianity of past ages.

There is another important point in Groethuysen's analysis to be mentioned—his observation that while the underlying categories of the new world vision (such as God, sin, life and death) were radically different from the traditional categories with the same names, the Church's actual idea of society was increasingly bound to strike a bourgeois involved in the economic activity of the modern world as irrelevant to his life and conduct.

The old Christian view of society rested on the division of men into 'rich' and 'poor', 'nobles' and 'common people'. These were the categories of a traditional society in which *birth* was the decisive factor in determining a man's social position. In such a society, wealth represented a responsibility, a duty and also a great peril to the Christian. The rich and mighty of the world were far more exposed to the temptations of power and pleasure than other people, and had much the harder task to resist them. In addition to this, the position in society which God had assigned to them for their earthly lives brought with it responsibility for their fellow men and the duty to help them. Alms-giving and charity were the chief means of rendering this aid, and were essential for the salvation of the soul.

As to the poor, they were required chiefly to endure their sufferings with patience as 'trials', and to regard purity of heart and simplicity of faith as the sure way to heaven.

This picture of society no longer made sense to the bourgeois of the eighteenth century. He saw wealth and comfort above all as the fruits of an energetic, successful life. Poverty and failure were generally the results of low intelligence or idleness. Charity on a large scale diminishing a family inheritance, such as had often been practised in the Middle Ages, now appeared to him as the despoiling of his own children and the renunciation of further possibilities of improvement in a life that he considered straightforward and even worthy—all this in order to help people who had worked less hard than their benefactor, and whose lives might not be above criticism. Poverty was perhaps not universally regarded as a sin, but it was no longer thought a condition pleasing to God.

This helps to explain the conflicts caused by the Church's attitude to trade and industry, and especially by the biblical ban on usury. In the traditional thought of the past, the search for profit and wealth was bound to be considered selfishly contrary to the general good and to concern for others. It was the unchristian life *par excellence*. The beginnings of bourgeois individualist society created a new, categorically opposite mental structure—the coincidence of private interest with public advantage—which later became a basic feature of the Enlightenment and the work of the classical economists. The economically active businessman or manufacturer not merely knew that—particular sins apart—he was leading an honourable and straightforward life; he also felt that, in becoming richer and improving his position, he was doing something useful and serving the public interest as well as his own.

In his view, the countries whose economies were the most advanced were those in which life was happiest and best; modern man was more fortunate than the primitive savage. This makes the campaign against the ban on usury easy to understand. The loan with which traditional doctrine was concerned, and on which the Bible forbade the charging of interest, was money lent for spending, given to a man fallen upon hard times through sickness or natural disaster to help him through the difficult first period of recovery. To demand interest on such a loan was to exploit the misfortune of a fellow man for one's own profit. In the modern society of the eighteenth century lending had become an entirely different matter. It was transformed from a loan of money for spending into a loan to finance production. This made it an essential factor of the economy. Money now was lent not to the poor to help them through a hard time, but to the rich for use in commercial transactions or investment in manufacture. Often enough even people of modest means lent money to the rich, with the new type of broker or bank as an intermediary, and derived some of their income from the interest. This made the traditional Christian ban on interest seem both anti-social and utterly senseless in modern society.

All this shows the difficulty facing the individualist in modern society in trying to adapt his life to the traditional Christian categories and fit them into his world vision as a guide to his thought and conduct.

It will be objected that Christianity has survived the attacks of the 'trial of God' and managed to retain its spiritual strength in western society to this day. No doubt there is some justice in the objection. But Christianity has been able to survive only because Christian belief itself changed and was adapted to the growth of a predominantly 'deconsecrated' area of modern life. Meanwhile bourgeois thought passed through its heroic period of development and found itself confronted with different problems, in whose solution religion proved to be a help. But these problems lie outside the scope of this section, which is concerned precisely with the 'heroic period' of the campaign of the Enlightenment against Christian belief.

Attacks on Christianity

Although the *philosophes* held different views on many subjects, including their concepts of religion, they were broadly in agreement in their attitude to Christianity and the Church. All of them, acting in the name of individual reason and the fundamental values of freedom, human equality, justice and toleration, put the Church and Christianity as a whole, together with every other positive religion, as it were on trial.

Whether they called themselves atheists, deists or theists, the *philosophes* considered it repulsive to reason that any given positive religion should be treated as *the true faith* or allowed to claim any privilege over other religions. Furthermore those of them that were not, or had not yet become, atheists demanded that a 'true' religion must be clearly true to all men, and must therefore not hold doctrines dependent on revelation and inaccessible to reason; above all these doctrines must not conflict with rational thought and rational bourgeois morality. It followed that any Church which advanced a positive religion became an object of suspicion, and it was considered the duty of a good government to deprive it of all political influence. By contrast the 'true' religion of Christ (in Voltaire) or of the Apostles (in Rousseau) more or less closely corresponds to the 'natural' religion founded on reason.

We will now use the words of Voltaire, Rousseau and Diderot to illustrate their views on Christianity and the Church. These

65

thinkers are the best-known representatives both of the Enlightenment itself and of the three main religious tendencies within the movement. The chief emphasis will be placed on Diderot in order to bring out how his views on these questions changed.

Voltaire Voltaire was a deist and believed in a good Creator and Architect of the Universe, whom he thought a friend to mankind. His thought concentrated on the battle against the intolerance and political influence of the Church and its priests. At the same time he fought all the irrational Christian dogmas that diverged from the morality and rational beliefs of natural religion. One can quote almost at random from his extensive writings on questions of religion and the Church.

The following extracts come from his *Dialogue du douteur et de l'adorateur*, in which Voltaire puts his own views into the mouth of the believer:

Doubter	How can you prove the existence of God?
Believer	Just as I would prove the existence of the sun—by opening my eyes.
Doubter	Do you also believe in final causes?
Believer	When I see an excellent effect I believe the cause to be excellent. God save me from being like the fool who said that a clock does not prove a clock maker. . . .
Doubter	What is your religion?
Believer	Not merely that of Socrates, who ridiculed the fables of the Greeks, but that of Jesus, who confounded the Pharisees. . . . Jesus founded no orders of Benedictines, Premonstratensians or Jesuits.
Doubter	Do you think one can serve God if one eats mutton on Fridays and never goes to mass?
Believer	Certainly I do, since Jesus never said mass, and ate meat on Fridays, and Saturdays as well.

Doubter Do you believe then that the religion of Jesus,
which was also evidently the religion of all
the sages of antiquity, has been corrupted?

Believer I think there is nothing more certain. He must
have been wise to speak against the false priests
and their superstitions. But he is credited with
things that no wise man could have said or
done. . . .

The conversation ends with the following declaration from the
Believer:

> My religion is that of all mankind, that of Socrates,
> of Plato, of Aristides, of Cicero, of Cato, of Titus,
> of Antoninus, of Marcus Aurelius, of Epictetus, of
> Jesus. . . . I combine qualities in myself, each of
> which imposes a duty on me: I am a man, a citizen
> of the world, a son of God, a brother to all men, a
> son, a husband, a father; all these name me, none is
> a dishonour. My duty is to praise God for
> everything, to thank him for everything, to bless
> him all the days of my life. . . . A hundred such
> maxims are worth no more than the Sermon on the
> Mount and that fine maxim, 'Blessed are the poor
> in spirit.' In short I shall worship God and not the
> deceit of men; I shall serve God and not a
> Council of Chalcedon or a Council *in Trullo*; I
> shall hate base superstition and shall be a strict
> follower of the true religion until my last breath.

The article on 'Priest' in Voltaire's *Dictionnaire philosophique*
begins thus:

> Priests in a state approach nearly to what preceptors are in
> private families. It is their province to teach, pray, and
> supply example. They ought to have no authority over the
> masters of the house; at least until it can be proved that he
> who gives the wages ought to obey him who receives them.

Of all religions, the one which most positively excludes the priesthood from civil authority is that of Jesus: 'Give unto Caesar the things which are Caesar's. . . . Among you there is neither first nor last. . . . My kingdom is not of this world.' The quarrels between the empires and the priesthood, which have bedewed Europe with blood for more than six centuries, have therefore been, on the part of priests, nothing but rebellion at once against God and man, and a continual sin against the Holy Ghost. . . . The Turks are wise in this; they religiously make a pilgrimage to Mecca, but they will not permit the Shereef of Mecca to excommunicate the Sultan. Neither will they purchase from Mecca permission not to observe the Ramadan, or the liberty of espousing their cousins or their nieces. They are not judged by Imams, whom the Shereef delegates; nor do they pay the first year's revenue to the Shereef. What is to be said of all that? Reader, speak for yourself.

In *Les Idées républicaines, par un membre d'un corps*, Voltaire writes:

The most absurd of despotisms, the most humiliating to human nature, the most contradictory, the most deadly, is that of priests. Of all priestly dominations, that of the priests of Christianity is beyond question the most criminal. It is an outrage to our Gospel, for Jesus says in twenty different places, 'Among you there is neither first nor last. My kingdom is not of this world. The Son of God came not to be served but to be a servant.' (V)

When our bishop, who is there to serve and not to be served, to comfort the poor and not to devour their substance, to teach the catechism and not to dominate, dared, in a time of disorder, to call himself the prince of a town of which he should be the shepherd, he was clearly guilty of rebellion and tyranny. (VI)

In this way the Bishops of Rome, who were the first to set this deadly example, made both their power and their sect detested in half of Europe; in this way several German bishops became more than once oppressors of the people to whom they should have been fathers. (VII)

In the *Dictionnaire philosophique* the section on Catechism contains a number of articles. One of them, 'The Catechism of the Japanese', compares different religions with different styles of cooking. The point is that everyone should be free to cook as he pleases. The king who rules the land will have an official style of cuisine, but he should not forbid his subjects to retain theirs, so long as they do not become rebellious or begin to threaten public order. The next article, 'The Gardener's Catechism', begins with a question from Tuctan to Karpos the gardener and ideal bourgeois: 'What is your present religion?' Karpos replies, 'My Pasha, it would be truly difficult to tell you.' He has lived under the rule of the Greeks, the Venetians and the Turks, and learned to believe a series of different doctrines, all unintelligible and equally trifling, and to pray in different ways.

Rousseau Within the thought of the Enlightenment Rousseau stands in sharp opposition to Voltaire and the Encyclopedists, and on many questions he adopts other, and sometimes opposite, views. His treatment of religion and the Church is quite different in tone from Voltaire's. He called himself a theist and had far greater respect and sympathy for the 'true' Christianity of the Gospels and the 'true' content of all positive religions, and even for priests, provided they were enlightened. But apart from that, the *theoretical* content of his views on religion, Christianity and the Church was closely related to that of Diderot and Voltaire. Like Voltaire and the young Diderot, Rousseau was a believer in natural religion, though his concept of the Divine Being cannot be reduced to that of the clock maker or architect. Like them he rejected all revelation, including that of Christianity, as contrary to reason. Like them he was a sharp critic of all intolerance and all

influence exerted by any positive religion on the government of
the state.

In the last part of his celebrated *Profession of Faith of a Savoyard
Vicar* Rousseau presents a detailed criticism of revelation in
general, and particularly Christian revelation. I quote from a
number of places.

The vicar explicitly warns Émile to attribute no authority to
his words save that of reason, and continues:

> Our grandest ideas of the Divine Nature come to us solely
> through reason. Behold the spectacle of nature. Listen to
> your inner voice. Has not God told everything to our eyes,
> our conscience and our reason? What can men tell us more?
> Their revelations serve only to degrade God, attributing
> human passions to him. . . . If there were a religion in the
> world that brought eternal damnation to those who did not
> believe, and if there were a sole mortal of good will who
> was not convinced of its truth, the God of this religion
> would be the most wicked and cruel of tyrants. . . . [The
> God] who destines the greatest number of his creatures to
> eternal punishment is not the good and merciful God that
> my reason has shown me. . . . Our Catholics make much of
> the authority of the Church; but what do they gain by this?
> . . . The Church decides that it has the right to decide.
> There is a well proved authority for you! . . . Some think it
> more important to make God unjust and punish the children
> for the sins of their fathers than to give up their barbarous
> dogma.

Continuing his exposition of the manner in which he fulfils
his duties, the priest explains that in his instruction he relies less
on the spirit of the Church than on that of the Gospels, 'where
the doctrine is simple and the morality is sublime, where there is
little religious practice and much charity'. In short he declares
that he does not claim authority to pronounce Christianity or any
other religion false, but that he recognizes only what reason and
sentiment show him to be just and moral.

In the last chapter of the *Social Contract*, which is headed 'Civil Religion', Rousseau discusses the relations between religion and the political order and distinguishes three types of religion: those of the man, the citizen and the priest. The last two, he says, acknowledge different authorities in society, that of the government and that of the Church:

> Politically each of these types of religion has its faults. The last is so obviously bad that it would be a waste of time to amuse oneself proving it. . . . The second is good in that it unites the worship of God with love of the laws, and in that it makes the nation the object of the people's worship and thus teaches them that to serve the state is to serve God, its protector. . . . But this religion is bad if it is founded on error and falsehood and deceives the people. . . . It is bad also if it becomes exclusive and tyrannical, making the people bloodthirsty and intolerant, so that men breathe murder and believe that they are doing something holy when they kill all who will not accept their gods. . . . There remains the religion of the man, or Christianity—not the Christianity of today but that of the Gospels, which is completely different. . . . But this religion has no connection with the body of the state. Indeed, far from attaching the hearts of the citizens to the state, it takes them away, as it detaches them from all earthly things. I can think of nothing more contrary to the social spirit.

For these reasons Rousseau proposes, in addition to the Gospel Christianity of the Savoyard Vicar, which comes close to natural religion, an official state religion, with its content limited to a small number of easily understood, precise and positive doctrines: the existence of an omnipotent, good, intelligent and far-seeing deity; life after death; happiness for the good and punishment for the evil; the sanctity of the social contract and the laws. There is to be only one negative doctrine: all forcing of conscience and all intolerance are to be forbidden.

Diderot Diderot is the most radical of the three. His views may be illustrated from works dating from four different periods of his life. We begin with the *Pensées philosophiques* written in 1746, when Diderot was still a deist. Two extracts have already been quoted on the tyrannical character of the Christian god. In contrast to these, a whole series of *pensées* emphasizes the physico-theological argument in favour of the natural religion of reason and the impossibility of understanding the purposive character of nature and the world if the existence of a creator outside the world is not acknowledged.

The superstitious and irrational character of Christianity and every positive religion results only in estranging rational men from faith, making them sceptics and atheists. On the other hand the contemplation of nature and its purposeful ordering proves the existence of a rational and good divine being.

> It is not the hand of the metaphysician that has struck the sharpest blows against atheism. The sublime meditations of Malebranche and Descartes were less capable of shaking materialism than a single observation of Malpighi's. If this dangerous hypothesis is weakened in our day, the credit is due to experimental physics. It is in the works of Newton, Musschenbroek, Hartsoeker and Nieuwentyt that we have found satisfactory proofs of the existence of a supremely intelligent Being. Thanks to the works of these great men, the world is no longer a god. Instead it is a machine, with its wheels, ropes, pulleys, springs and weights. (XVIII)

> The subtleties of ontology have at the best produced sceptics. It was reserved for the knowledge of nature to produce true deists. (XIX)

In numerous *pensées* Diderot defends scepticism, and in doing so is clearly upholding his own position:

> It is fair to require me to seek the truth, but not to find it. . . . What have I to fear if I fall into error innocently? There is no reward in the next world for showing

intelligence in this one. Ought we to be punished then for lacking it? To condemn a man for bad reasoning is to forget that he is a fool and to treat him as a criminal. (XXIX)

What is a sceptic? He is a philosopher who has questioned all his beliefs, and believes only what the legitimate use of his reason and his senses shows him to be true. (XXX)

When the pious declaim against scepticism, it seems to me that they do not fully understand their own interests, or that they are contradicting themselves. If it is certain that a true religion need only be properly known to be adopted, and a false faith need only be understood to be rejected, it must be highly desirable that universal doubt should spread over the face of the earth, and every race be willing to question the truth of its religion. Our missionaries would find a good half of their work done for them. (XXXVI)

The last sentence of course is ironic, but at the time of the *Pensée philosophiques* Diderot was still convinced that scepticism, as a radical and critical mode of thought (which he distinguished from Pyrrhonism: 'Make a Pyrrhonist sincere and you have the sceptic'), while questioning all positive religion, would inevitably create awareness of the truth of natural religion with its 'all-wise, all-good clock maker'.

Pensée LXII, which closes the volume, illustrates this view. After repeatedly criticizing the claim made by every positive religion to be the sole repository of truth, Diderot writes:

I hear cries of impiety on all sides. In Asia a Christian is an infidel, in Europe a Mohammedan, in London a Papist, in Paris a Calvinist. At the upper end of the Rue Saint-Jacques [the site of the Jesuit college of Louis le Grand] a Jansenist is an unbeliever, a Molinist is one in the Faubourg Saint-Médard. Well, what is an unbeliever? Is it everybody or nobody? (XXXV)

This leads him to conclude:

This diversity of opinions has led the deists to adopt a form of argument that is perhaps more curious than substantial. Cicero, having to show that the Romans were the most warlike people in the world, draws this admission from the lips of their rivals. Gauls, if you acknowledged a superior in courage, who would it be? The Romans. Parthians, who are the bravest nation after you? The Romans. Africans, whom would you fear, if you feared any? The Romans. Let us follow his example, say the deists, and question the believers of all other faiths. O Chinese, what religion would be the best if it were not your own? Natural religion. Mohammedans, what faith would you embrace if you abjured Mahomet? Natural religion. Christians, what is the true faith, if it is not Christianity? Judaism. But you, O Jews, what say you is the true religion if Judaism is false? Natural religion. Now, continues Cicero, those whom all are agreed in placing second, and who do not yield first place to another, have an undoubted claim to be placed first themselves. (LXII)

That was Diderot's view in 1746. Twenty-four years later, in 1770, he wrote a new set of *Pensées* which were printed in nearly all editions under the title *Addition aux Pensées philosophiques*. Now there is no more talk of natural religion and deism. The text is an attack on *every* sort of religion, particularly on Christianity. Diderot had become a thoroughgoing atheist. Not only the content but also the manner had become much sharper. I quote almost at random:

Doubt in religious matters, far from being a form of impiety, ought to be considered good, since it is the act of a man who humbly acknowledges his own ignorance, and since it springs from the fear of displeasing God by the abuse of reason. (I)

If reason is the gift of heaven, and if the same can be said of faith, then heaven has given us two gifts that are not only incompatible but in contradiction to one another. (V)

To escape this difficulty we must say that faith is a chimera and has no existence in nature. (VI)

The god of the Christians is a father who makes a great to do about his apples and little about his children. (XVI)

To prove the Gospel by means of a miracle is to prove the absurd by means of the impossible. (XXI)

Why are the miracles of Christ true, and those of Aesculapius, Apollonius of Tyana and Mahomet false? (XXIV)

This God, who lets God die to appease God is an excellent phrase of la Hontan's. The evidence for and against Christianity of a hundred folio volumes is worth less than the laughter of these few words. (XL)

This body rots, this blood turns sour. This god is consumed by the maggots on his altar. Blind nation, Egyptian imbecile, open your eyes! (XXX)

Are not the precepts of religion and the laws of society really absurd and cruel to forbid murder of the innocent? By killing them one ensures their eternal bliss; in letting them live one condemns them almost certainly to perpetual misery. (LXX)

Lastly an isolated fragment entitled *Pensée philosophique*:

A man had been betrayed by his children, his wife and his friends. Treacherous partners had destroyed his fortune and made him destitute. Filled with hatred and deep contempt for the human race, he left society and took refuge in a solitary cavern. There, pressing his fists into his eyes, and planning a revenge proportioned to his bitterness, he said, 'Monsters! What shall I do to punish their acts of injustice and make them as wretched as they deserve? Ah, were it but possible to imagine . . . to put into their heads an illusion,

75

which they would think more important than their own lives, on which they could never agree with each other!' . . . At that moment he rushed out of the cavern crying 'God! God! . . .' Countless echoes all around him repeated 'God! God!' The terrifying name was carried from pole to pole, and everywhere it was heard with astonishment. Men at first fell down to worship, then they rose, asked questions, argued, became embittered, cursed one another, hated one another, and cut one another's throats. Thus was the deadly wish of the hater of mankind fulfilled. For such has been the past history, and such will be the future, of a being who is important and incomprehensible alike.

Diderot's transition from the *Pensées philosophiques* to the *Addition* suggests a crucial theoretical change, particularly in his answer to the question, that in 1746 had seemed the decisive argument in favour of deism, about the maker of the wonderful 'machine' of the Cosmos and its component parts, especially living creatures.

Diderot in fact moved to a form of immanent pantheism resting principally on the idea that matter in all its forms possesses a potential capacity for sensation, which shows outwardly only in living creatures. The great argument in favour of this hypothesis is the process by which dead matter is constantly transmuted into living matter by means of assimilation. The argument is set forth in his celebrated trilogy, *Entretien entre d'Alembert et Diderot*; *Le Rêve de d'Alembert*; *Suite de l'entretien*. In the first section Diderot gives an exposition of his hypothesis to d'Alembert, using the subsequently famous parallel between a man (especially a philosopher) and a harpsichord, endowed with memory and the ability to play music without the presence of a musician. In the perspective of this analogy, the living organism, which had previously been Diderot's strongest argument for the existence of God, becomes the main ground of attack on all faith and theology. When Diderot has explained the comparison between the philosopher and the harpsichord, d'Alembert replies:

I understand. So if this harpsichord which has feeling and life possessed also the power to feed itself and reproduce its kind, it would live and breed of itself, or with the female of its species, little living, playing harpsichords.

Diderot Undoubtedly. What else, in your view is a chaffinch, a nightingale, a musician, or a man? What other difference is there between a canary and a serinette.[1] Do you see this egg? With its aid we can overturn all the schools of theology and all the temples in the world. What is this egg? An unfeeling mass, before the germ is introduced. And after the introduction of the germ, what is it still? Still an unfeeling mass, for this seed itself is but a passive and impercipient fluid. How will this mass pass to another state of organism—to feeling, to life? By heat. What will produce heat? Movement. . . .

In this way the hypothesis of potential feeling in matter becomes Diderot's theoretical basis for radical atheism.

The division of the text into three parts is entirely logical. In the first section Diderot expounds the theory itself to d'Alembert. In the second, d'Alembert, in the presence of his friend Mademoiselle de l'Espinasse and Dr Bordeu, dreams about possible scientific theories and discoveries based on the hypothesis—theories that had partly been formulated in Diderot's time and partly were not worked out till later.

Finally in the third part Mademoiselle de l'Espinasse discusses the moral consequences of this form of atheism with Bordeu; they consider the assertion that anything useful or merely pleasant is permissible so long as it is not harmful. The concrete results reached by the speakers are slightly unexpected.

Before leaving Diderot I wish to mention one further small piece written by him, a dialogue between the philosophical

---

[1] Miniature organ used for teaching canaries to sing particular tunes. In the original there is an untranslatable pun on *serin*, canary.

atheist and a lady of high society. Its title is *Entretien d'un philosophe avec la Maréchale de* ——. The lady is thought to be the niece of the financier Samuel Bernard and the wife of Marshal de Broglie; she thus belonged to that highest section of the bourgeoisie which was already beginning to merge with the nobility. 'She is as beautiful and pious as an angel . . . she thought that anyone who denied the Trinity was a ruffian who would end on the gallows.'

The Maréchale is surprised to learn that Diderot can be an unbeliever and still lead the life of a decent Christian, and is neither thief nor brigand nor murderer. 'What then do you gain by not believing?' she asks in astonishment. This leads the philosopher to ask if people believe because there is something to be gained by it.

'I do not know,' she replies, 'but a little self-interest comes in useful both for this world and the next.' Later she accuses the philosopher of being inconsistent:

Diderot	Why so?
The Maréchale	Because I think that, if I had nothing to hope or fear after death, there are a good many little pleasures in this world that I should not deny myself. I admit that I lend to God at a stiff rate of interest.
Diderot	For my part I never expect any return on my money.
The Maréchale	All beggars are in that situation.
Diderot	You would rather I were a usurer?
The Maréchale	Why, yes. One can practise usury with God as much as one pleases; he will not be ruined by it. I know that it is hardly the thing, but what does that matter? As the essential thing is to get into heaven, whether by craft or by force, one must use every means and neglect no source of profit. . . . Do you then really expect nothing?

Diderot	Nothing.
The Maréchale	How sad! But you must admit that you are either a rogue or a madman. . . . What motive can an unbeliever have for being good unless he be mad? . . .
Diderot	Do you not think it possible to be born with such a happy disposition as to find real pleasure in doing good? . . . That an excellent education may strengthen this disposition? . . . That in later life experience may have convinced us that on the whole it serves our worldly happiness better to be an honest man than to be a rogue?

The Maréchale accepts all this, but asks what happens if passion draws the unbeliever into wickedness:

Diderot	He is inconsistent. Is there anything more common than inconsistency?
The Maréchale	Alas, unfortunately not. People believe, yet every day behave as if they did not.
Diderot	And without believing, one behaves very much as if one did. . . .
The Maréchale	If you like; but what can be the harm in having one reason the more—religion—for doing good, and one reason the less— unbelief—for doing wrong?
Diderot	None at all, if religion were a motive for doing good and lack of faith for doing wrong.

Further on we meet all the familiar arguments used by Diderot against Christianity in the *Pensées philosophiques* and elsewhere. The Maréchale brings in the usefulness of religion in keeping the 'people' from wickedness. Diderot replies that religion may induce her steward to steal a little less just before Easter than just after. But, through intolerance and religious wars, faith has brought evil into the world out of all proportion to the undoubted good it has done. The Maréchale objects that these are abuses (not the essentials) of religion. 'If abuses and essentials are inseparable,' replies Diderot, 'the abuse must be considered part of religion.'

He continues that it is a matter of complete indifference whether people are Christian or pagan, and repeats the remark quoted earlier that there are no more real Christians. 'It would be enough,' he adds, 'for twenty thousand Parisians to take it into their heads to base their conduct strictly on the Sermon on the Mount. . . . There would be so many lunatics that the Chief of Police would be at a loss to find room for them in the asylums.'

He explains to the Maréchale how priests forbid totally harmless acts much more strenuously than those that harm others. It is not his aim, he says, to make converts or prevent anyone from believing it possible to see without eyes, hear without ears or think without a head. But he cannot understand why, if a spirit created the material world, it should be thought impossible for matter to create spirit.

The discussion continues with the observation that if God judged justly, mortals would have no more grounds for fearing his judgement than his non-existence. Diderot means that if there is a God, he can fortunately not be angry with a philosopher for doubting his existence when there are no grounds for believing in it.

After a parable on this theme, Diderot asks the Maréchale if her husband would refuse to forgive one of their children who had misbehaved. She objects that God and her husband are two quite different things, and Diderot asks in astonishment whether she means that her husband is better than God. 'God forbid!' she answers. 'I mean only that my justice is not the same as my husband's, and his is not the same as God's.' Diderot then ends the conversation by saying that he cannot conceive a justice that is not one and the same for all; but he has enough love of his neighbour to keep his opinions secret from magistrates if need be, in order to 'spare them from performing a brutal act'.

These quotations make all commentary superfluous. They are a summary of all the criticisms of Christianity made by *philosophes* of every tendency, criticisms not of an imaginary Christianity but of the real religion of their times. Here again we have a verification of the fundamental dialectical principle that if what is thought about a situation expresses historical progress (as the Enlightenment did) the thought is itself a part of the situation.

Alienation

Western society was in the process of organizing itself rationally and was giving a constantly growing importance in life to the autonomous intellect. This process made the intellect seem not only the means of escape from a world vision that had been alive and in accord with reason in the past, but also a weapon against the surviving remains of that world vision, which had tried in vain to adapt itself to modern society and consequently become absurd and contrary to reason.

But Diderot had reached the limits of the Enlightenment. None of the *philosophes* was so conscious of the weaknesses and inadequacies of the movement. As Hegel put it, the *Encyclopédie*, in becoming a sort of 'sum' of knowledge and understanding, pointed beyond the Enlightenment in asking for the meaning of such knowledge in terms of its human content. This raises—not in Diderot but in later writers—the question, with which Goethe opens *Faust*, about the revival of religion and faith, and paradoxical though it may seem, about the ending of human 'estrangement'.

Philosophical writing, particularly the secondary literature, has generally seen estrangement in its religious form and thus used 'the overcoming of estrangement' to mean 'the overcoming of religious thought'.

Hegel still knew that, in genuine belief, even in an unauthentic, 'ideological' form, man could find himself in the God in whom he believed. Belief accordingly became 'intuition' and 'superstition' only with the development of rationalism.

Marx, in his remarkable scientific analysis, showed how the economic life of capitalism simultaneously created the first basically non-believing, deconsecrated society and the most acute form of human alienation. These two phenomena seem intimately connected.

Working from this, modern man asks how far he can overcome estrangement, rediscover a purely humanist and immanent faith, and thus attain the synthesis of intellect, faith and immanence which, in its ultimate tendency, if not by strict derivation, corresponds with what classical German philosophy calls *Vernunft* (reason).

History is irreversible, and it seems impossible that Christianity should ever again become the mode in which men really live and think. None the less, this question remains at the centre of modern intellectual life, which is more than ever dominated in all its important forms of expression by the problem of the absence of the divine. Are we to have a secular, technologically advanced, and totally rational society? Or is the community of men, while taking over the technological opportunities developed by bourgeois society and developing them further, at the same time to overcome estrangement and create a new, immanent, non-transcendental religious outlook on human society and history?

The 'judgement of history' has passed Christianity by. Diderot's argument that modern society makes it impossible for anyone to give a genuinely Christian character to his whole life is more valid than ever today. The more sincere and intense the Christian life of modern man, the more it becomes a purely inward, psychological 'private matter' deprived of all influence on life in society.

The two world visions between which the judgement of history must decide today are still the same visions of 'knowledge' and 'faith' in modern dress. We have to choose between morally neutral technical knowledge and the synthesis of knowledge with immanent faith in a human community to be created by men; between understanding (*Verstand*) and reason (*Vernunft*); between capitalism and socialism. It is for us to determine which of these is to be the future vision of mankind.

III The Enlightenment and the Problems of Modern Society

The critique of the Enlightenment by means of the dialectic seemed to many educated people, particularly the socialists of the generation before ours, one of the decisive achievements of western intellectual history. After the decline of neo-Kantianism, which was largely a reversion to the individualist mental categories of the Enlightenment, there seemed to be scarcely a serious rationalist left in Europe. Those that remained were either, like Ernst Cassirer, the last remnants of a bygone period of philosophy, or isolated figures with no claim to any influence on the structure of European intellectual life.

There are two completely separate intellectual positions which are often confused in discussions of the critique or 'overthrow' of the Enlightenment. One is bourgeois thought, which, since the revival of interest in Kierkegaard early in this century (and this revival must be understood as a symptom, not a cause), has lost its optimism and confident belief in the individual and adopted opposite, irrational categories. The other is dialectical materialism, which continues the development of the humanist tradition of German idealism in a positive scientific form.

The 'internal crisis'

There can be no doubt that, if we are to understand modern capitalist society and western intellectual life, we must revise and refine the accepted Marxist analysis. None the less the Marxist concept of an 'internal crisis' in bourgeois society and thought seems genuinely applicable to the period between 1914 and 1945 in western Europe as a whole, and especially in Germany.

That is the period which saw the growth of a world vision (which requires further and closer structural analysis) characterized, *despite its retention of the individualist perspective*, by its view of the individual as dominated by dread and the feeling of 'dereliction', especially in his utter powerlessness to understand or master the world around him.

In the perspective of this vision, the confident, optimistic thought of the Enlightenment, especially its hostility to religion, came to seem superficial and limited. The bourgeoisie had already become a force for conservatism in the nineteenth century and moved from its former anti-Christian position to take up a much more favourable attitude towards religion as a 'support for the existing social order'; in the first half of the twentieth century, under the pressure of inner instability and anxiety, it turned to a subjectively sincere, and sometimes even ultra-religious, form of belief; but in comparison with the faith of the true ages of religion, this new kind of faith was not objectively authentic. It had no substantial content, but was a mere expression of subjective experience, and therefore almost without effect on society.

The crisis of this period seems to have been caused by the economic threat to society, which did not become apparent in its full dimensions until the great depression of 1929–33, but was the underlying ground of all that took place between 1914 and 1945. Accordingly if we now speak of a *new* intellectual situation, that is not because Kierkegaard and Heidegger have ceased to be completely relevant to us, but because, since 1945, western capitalist society appears to have worked out a series of methods of regulating the economy, by means of which it has averted the danger of large-scale economic crisis. Although there are inevitably still moments of social and political danger, these are not of a fundamental sort, as they were in the first half of the century.

Despite the external threat of the socialist nations and the movement towards independence of the underdeveloped countries, despite the occasional shocks and fever symptoms accompanying the end of colonialism, western society is in the process of recovering from the most serious of its inner sicknesses, and is thus taking away the foundation of ideologies based on anxiety and despair.

In these circumstances the retreat from reason into inner, individualist religiosity comes to seem a delayed subjective survival from a bygone social and intellectual situation; it can no longer be seen as a mode of thought and experience that genuinely points to the future of bourgeois society.

This situation perhaps makes it easier to see that there have been several periods in the history of bourgeois thought that could be described as reversions to the perspective of the Enlightenment. The first seems to be the early post-Hegelian period, between Hegel himself and the development of Marxism. Marx's own first writings show distinct traces of Enlightenment thought: his doctoral thesis is a panegyric of Epicurus, 'the great Enlightenment philosopher of antiquity'. There is another such period in the second half of the nineteenth century, when neo-Kantian philosophers, though nominally returning to Kant, in reality returned to Fichte.

The bond between the bourgeoisie and Enlightenment seems to be *fundamental*, even though it was temporarily broken in times of crisis like the early period of German idealist philosophy or the years between 1914 and 1945. But we must add that even in such periods of crisis the rationalist position was not entirely abandoned. For example, it is precisely the combination of rationalism with awareness of crisis that is the most distinctive feature of the work of Paul Valéry.

If this is true, we may assume with a fair degree of probability that—given success in achieving disarmament and ending the danger of atomic war—western society is moving towards another great period of Enlightenment. This coming period will, like its predecessors, be no mere repetition of the past, but will have its own specific forms.[1]

[1] It is a characteristic symptom that there has been a vast increase in the various series of pocket editions of books on scientific and philosophical questions. These

Thus the 'overthrow of the Enlightenment' by inward, individualist and irrational religious belief, as in philosophers like Bergson, Heidegger, Jaspers, Jean Wahl and Gabriel Marcel, seems ultimately to have been a mere passing phase in the intellectual history of western society, which history is already rendering obsolete, and over which we need spend no more time.

Marxist criticism

The question of the relation between the Enlightenment and the dialectical thought prevailing in the intellectual life of much of the world today is more serious and of greater objective, as well as subjective, importance.

As I have shown, dialectical consciousness began in Hegel and Goethe with a radical critique of individualism, especially in its Enlightenment form. The Being of man is not fully exhausted in knowledge; knowledge is but an element in a totality which must have some substantial content. This view is most effectively expressed in Goethe's famous scene where Faust, wishing to translate the opening of St John's Gospel into his 'beloved German', rejects in turn the renderings 'Word', 'Reason' and 'Force', and at last finds the only proper translation: 'In the beginning was the Act.'

For the immanent pantheist vision of the dialectic there is only one substantial content: man himself. But if man becomes the consciously known content of human action, if man is at the same time the subject and object of action, then neither subject

---

are in essence the *Encyclopédie* in modern dress. The only difference is that, in keeping with the changed social situation, these books express no coherent philosophical view of the world. Another symptom is the great success, especially in English-speaking countries, of K. R. Popper's *The Open Society*. On the other hand there is Sartre's *La Nausée*, published in 1938 at the height of the Existentialist period. The book is anti-rationalist and anti-humanist. The self-educated man in it, who reads his way through the books in the public library in alphabetical order, is certainly a satirical character; but the satire is directed at one of the Enlightenment's central beliefs—that knowledge could be transmitted in alphabetically arranged sections through the medium of the *Encyclopédie* and the dictionaries.

nor object can any longer be the individual. The individual can have only things—or other people treated as things—as the object of his action. The object of action must, then, be *the community of men*. If, in its turn, the human community, acting through the individuals of whom it is composed, makes itself the object of its action, then its action is conscious history.

Dialectical thought conceives man as a historical being who constantly transcends his nature through action[1] and thus moves towards the only possible conjunction of the human and the divine, the reconciliation of man and nature in conscious history, which is the one and only realization of freedom.

In this system of philosophy the people of the past are of course seen as historical subjects too; but they were not conscious of their essential nature, and made history in an ideological, 'alienated' form. Their actions too had human society for their content, but as men remained unconscious of this, they gave the content the status of an absolute, thought of it in an alienated form outside themselves, and called it God. The great periods of human history are those in which men, though acting unconsciously and in ideological form, came close to this real content, finding themselves in God and God in themselves. These were the true ages of faith.

By dissolving all the bonds of the human community and eliminating them from the individual consciousness, bourgeois society deprived human thought and feeling of all content.

While the development of the bourgeoisie retained a historically progressive function, its members could feel, without explicitly knowing it, that the purely formal thought of their society, like the faith of the Middle Ages, had an actual, even if implicit, substantial (and therefore historical) content. Accordingly the ideological thought of the eighteenth century, and the individualist vision of the bourgeoisie, in its entire period of development over several centuries, were as substantial and authentic as the faith of the great ages of religion.

This led to the situation so aptly described by Hegel. The

[1] Pascal's definition: 'L'homme passe infiniment l'homme.'

Enlightenment, having attainèd self-awareness and established the autonomy of human understanding chiefly by depriving this understanding of genuine content, was battling against a religion and a religious outlook that in reality embodied another form of itself: the same consciousness, based on the same intellectual categories, though perverted into the form of false, reactionary superstition.

German idealism, and its developments in dialectical philosophy and socialism were an expression of hope—since the triumph of the bourgeoisie had deprived rationalist thought of all progressive meaning—that some way might be found of replacing the alternatives of false, unhistorical rationalism or spurious religion with a new immanent faith in which mankind would consciously assume responsibility for its progress and development as the results of its own actions.

European intellectual life was then dominated by the crucial opposition between the pseudo-Christian, radically secularized bourgeois society, with its constantly growing, morally neutral economic life, and the immanent humanist faith of socialism, with its hope of an authentic intellectual and religious rebirth in the struggle for a future community, transparent and freed from ideology, to be created by men for themselves.

This was the situation in which the long development of the socialist critique of bourgeois thought took place. Its main content was the theory of alienation, taken from Hegel. In its scientific Marxist formulation this became the theory of commodity fetishism and reification.

The socialist theorists were right to point out that capitalism had for the first time in history created a fundamentally secularized society in which an economy indifferent to the distinction between divine and demonic, good and evil, beautiful and ugly, gained ground irresistibly; that in such a society the idea of mankind as a community would vanish together with all social feeling further and further from the individual consciousness, finding expression only in 'reified' form as an additional quality of goods, the 'price', and that this would then become the sole determinant of human relations in economic life. They were right to point out that such a society splits the human personality, making the same man both a class-conscious bourgeois and a citizen of his nation, concerned, at least in theory, for the welfare of society as a whole; that it then further splits the individual bourgeois into two fundamentally opposed forms: the 'economic man', amoral, unfeeling and irreligious when he is earning his living, and the kind father, affectionate friend and good Christian in the rest of his life. Hence the myth of the werewolf and the story of Dr Jekyll and Mr Hyde perfectly symbolize modern man; and this myth has been used by great artists in our own times, for instance by Brecht in *The Good Woman of Sezuan* and by Chaplin in his film *Monsieur Verdoux*.

The socialists were right to argue that while capitalist society apparently realized the essential values of the Enlightenment, notably freedom, equality before the law and toleration, this realization was purely formal. In reality economic inequality and exploitation concealed the existence of major restrictions on freedom, equality and toleration. The intellectual life of bourgeois society was constantly becoming emptier and less capable of satisfying human needs. At the same time the fundamental values of brotherhood, community and hope for the future (apart from the poor, shrunken hope that the children would in time have a life like that of their parents) were gradually disappearing from human consciousness. To this was added the assertion that bourgeois society could not even give all its members a secure economic existence, and that the material welfare of the working class would be in ever greater danger.

Socialist thought contrasted this dismal picture with the hope of a new brotherhood, and a future for mankind as a whole, a revival of the spirit born of the workers' radical opposition to bourgeois society.

The Enlightenment had foundered on its very success in realizing its values. In the bourgeois world Christianity had become a private matter and, more often than not, a lie. Socialism seemed to be the only hope of economic and spiritual salvation.

Western society

That was the intellectual world in which our generation grew up. But then came the real historical events which forced us to make fundamental changes in many parts of this analysis. None the less, many important points in it were shown to be justified, and these same events revealed the menace latent in the moral neutrality of the capitalist economy, which proved, when it was in danger, as willing to join forces with fascism and barbarism as with the most civilized forms of democracy.

In the eighteenth century the work of the Marquis de Sade stands beside that of Diderot, Rousseau, Voltaire and d'Holbach to warn us of the ultimate possibilities of rationalism. In the same way German National Socialism confirmed the dangerous potential permanently present in a morally neutral economic life.

In addition to this, quite apart from fascism and barbarism, the emptiness of bourgeois intellectual life became increasingly evident in the modern movement in literature and art. The one great literary form created by bourgeois society, the novel, was an epic form which treated values only in terms of 'problems' (which explains the problematic nature of all the really great leading characters like Don Quixote, Julien Sorel and Emma Bovary); but contemporary literature from Kafka to Robbe-Grillet, Beckett, Adamov and Ionesco, like the modern style of painting which has abandoned all representation of reality and turned to pure abstraction, is above all a shocked, and often shocking, statement of the lack of values and emptiness of human life today.

The thirty years' 'crisis of bourgeois society' between 1914 and 1945 was punctuated by a number of violent social upheavals. First there was the victory of the socialist revolution in Russia in 1917 and the development of a socialist society continuing until the end of the second world war. This was followed by the success of the revolution in China and Yugoslavia and the spread of socialism to a large area of central Europe.

We should certainly not equate socialism with Stalinism, or

even with the totalitarian form of state in general, any more than we should equate capitalism with the dictatorship of Hitler, or bourgeois society with enlightened despotism. Socialism and capitalism are fundamental social structures, the others are the transient political forms in which they find expression, with a duration determined by circumstances and with the ability to transform themselves, to vanish and to reappear.

The reign of terror under Stalin was principally the result of a concrete historical situation: the external threat to an industrially, and therefore militarily, backward socialist state from the hostile and overwhelmingly stronger capitalist world. This analysis is confirmed by the fact that, when this situation had been basically changed by the success of the Chinese revolution and the achievement of military equality in the 'balance of terror' of atomic weapons, the destalinization of the Soviet state and society was begun without civil war or external defeat.

No doubt it is the fact that socialism has gained ground particularly in the less developed countries, that have no capitalist past, and consequently no bourgeois-democratic traditions anchored in the intellectual life of their society, that has contributed most to making its emphasis on the collective interest and its comparative disregard of the individual seem especially prominent.

But while it is important to keep all this in mind, it remains true that the experience of forty years of socialist society proves that the abolition of exchange and market production in a society with an economy entirely planned by the central authority poses a most serious threat to freedom, equality, toleration—all the great values of the Enlightenment.

Although these values have been rightly stigmatized in the socialist camp as purely formal and devoid of content; although freedom loses much of its meaning when it becomes, as Anatole France put it, 'freedom for the millionaire to sleep in a palace and for the beggar to make his bed under a bridge', and when those who have the money have the power to direct public opinion by means of the Press, the radio and every medium of propaganda;

although equality is critically weakened if it becomes mere equality 'before the law' and has no economic reality; although toleration is practised only in the domain of religion, since religion plays no significant part in the capitalist world; despite all this, western people in general, and particularly the educated classes, even the socialists among them, have become aware of the immense importance to human life of preserving the values of the Enlightenment.

The right to express and defend opinions in all social and political circumstances, in books and newspapers; respect for all men as possessing equal rights in law; toleration in religion and social philosophy: these give the life of society a fundamental structure which, even if realized only in formal terms, represents an immeasurable historical advance that cannot and must not lightly be thrown away.

But we must constantly emphasize that these values, though based on the market economy of western society, can be realized even in formal terms only so long as the economy maintains a relative equilibrium. At the first sign of crisis they are put in abeyance or abolished altogether; and this has already happened more than once. Besides this, western bourgeois society has undergone a number of decisive changes in the past thirty years. The pressure of economic crisis, of external politics, and of the much faster growth in production in the socialist world have led the west to give up some of the private character of its economic life and nationalize a considerable sector of its activity. In the same period a number of regulating devices have been introduced into the economy, enabling it to function smoothly with as little friction as possible.

Without making any claim to powers of prophecy, one can reasonably predict that—provided there is no outbreak of war, and provided the threat of war is removed—western society will be able to function and continually re-create itself without danger from any economic threat. (The sociological reasons for these changes are of course a problem of great importance, but cannot be considered in this study.)

In the course of this development western society has put a halt to two processes which the traditional Marxist analysis thought characteristic of capitalism: the proletarianization of the middle and lower bourgeoisie and the total pauperization of the working class. As a result a radical transformation of the Marxist analysis has been made necessary, and at the same time the ground has been cut away from under one of the most important of the socialist criticisms of the capitalist system. There is now an upward movement in the standard of living of the working class. This improvement, though it may not be as great as that experienced by other classes, is an absolute one. Wages may constitute a decreasing portion of the total national income, but their real value increases with growth in total output. Furthermore the middle classes are not disappearing; on the contrary, they have not only retained both their relative position and their absolute importance but have actually increased these. In addition, the introduction of automation and the discovery of new sources of power make it probable that in the not too distant future, possibly after some difficulties of transition and adaptation that we must certainly not underestimate, these processes will be intensified and transformed in their structural and qualitative importance.[1]

When the situation is considered in a wider historical perspective, we begin to see the outline of a possibility in modern western capitalism of securing for all the members of society, workers, lower and middle bourgeoisie and capitalists alike, a *relatively* high standard of living with the capacity in many cases to rise still higher. If the problems created by external dangers could be solved, we could take it that such a society, functioning more or less without friction and ensuring the general welfare, would also guarantee in large measure the freedom of the individual,

---

[1] It is *possible* that, with automation and the use of atomic energy, the enormous increase in productivity and the changed qualifications required by workers will change the relative strengths of the social classes in such a way that, by non-revolutionary methods of reformed management and control of production, society will move towards major limitations on the private ownership of the means of production and an extension of workers' participation in industrial policy-making and administration. This would indicate a fundamental change in the structure of society and an approach to the Yugoslavian pattern.

equality before the law, and toleration. In this way western capitalist society, which in the nineteenth century achieved only a part of the programme of the Enlightenment, is now ready to lay the foundations for the completion of the programme.

Because the values of formal freedom, equality and toleration are menaced in socialist societies (and we must hope and believe that the menace is only a passing danger), western thinkers, both bourgeois and socialist, have come to see that the picture of the world adopted by the Enlightenment should be judged neither totally obsolete nor irrelevant, but that it enshrines values of crucial importance whose preservation is one of the most urgent of the problems facing socialism.

In the socialist society of the future, Marx saw the heritage and continuation of bourgeois humanism. It has now become clear, however, that with the suppression of the market economy, which provides the basis of bourgeois society, the principal values of its humanism are endangered too. Socialist politicians and theorists who wish to remain loyal to the spirit of Marx are thus obliged to answer the question how socialism can transplant these values and realize them in a different form of society.

Towards a synthesis

Modern ideas on the 'obsolescence' of the Enlightenment are accordingly different from those held by the philosophers of the generation before ours. But at the same time the view of man taken by modern western society, even as we come closer to realizing the values of the Enlightenment, is now completely different from anything expected by the thinkers of the Enlightenment in their optimistic view of the future.

The criticisms by Hegel and Marx of the lack of content in the thought of the Enlightenment seemed in their time purely philosophical; they have now come to stand for one of the most urgent problems in the life of modern capitalist society.

In the seventeenth and eighteenth centuries the bourgeoisie contrived to empty traditional religious belief of all content, transform it into superstition, drive it out of the life of the community and confine it to the individual, and within the individual to exclude it from his life as a whole and confine it entirely to his private life. In the same way modern capitalist society in the West has succeeded in halting the absolute pauperization of the working class (this being the most important revision needed in Marxist theory), and in integrating the most important sections of the proletariat; by this success it has increasingly torn away the foundations of the new humanist religion that had begun to develop in the struggle between the working class and bourgeois society.

The western world is now engaged in constructing a fundamentally secular and deconsecrated industrial society. This is a society in which—if it is achieved—all men will live in comfort. Perhaps there will also be a large measure of formal freedom and religious and philosophical toleration. But it is a society that threatens to deprive human life of all spiritual content, a society in which the growth of freedom is likely to be accompanied by the growth in numbers of those whose inner emptiness robs them of the desire to use it, a society in which religious and philosophical toleration will be made all the easier to achieve as spiritual impoverishment makes religious and philosophical commitment constantly more rare.

Artists and thinkers are today becoming aware of these changes and beginning to struggle against them. Since the nineteen-twenties the meaninglessness of life and the absence of human values have been the most important theme of the great expressions of our intellectual life—in the work of Kafka, Musil, Heidegger and Jaspers. Modern French literature has taken up the theme and treated it, almost without horror or terror, as simple statement of fact. Ionesco's best plays portray a world in which intelligible human conversation simply does not exist. Beckett's one theme is the meaningless, godless world in which only a miracle keeps some small traces of human warmth alive. Robbe-Grillet's novels are set in a world where men and inanimate objects are no longer distinguishable from each other.

Some important thinkers see the inner structure of this self-stabilizing western capitalist society as a sort of 'end to history'. It may be called heaven or hell with equal aptness, for heaven and hell are alike facets of non-human, unhistorical existence.

I myself do not think that such views can yet be considered justified. It is impossible for a present-day prophet to make any definite predictions of what effect the great technical and economic changes of the near future will have on the social and intellectual life of the two dominant types of modern society. In the west they *may* lead to a soulless industrialized social structure, capable of raising standards of living to a very high level, but with no place for world visions and their philosophical and artistic expression. But it is also possible that the responsibility for production and for social and political action may pass into the hands of all the members of society, and this could open up the prospect of a rebirth of historical and intellectual life in a framework in which the traditional values of the individual conscience would be safeguarded and freedom and toleration assured.

Likewise there are decisive changes taking place in the socialist states. The social experiment of Yugoslavia, though not of the first political or historical importance, has great significance in the perspective of philosophy and social theory. This is so chiefly because it is an attempt to combine the abolition of the private ownership of the means of production with the maintenance of a market economy. This attempt may perhaps lay the foundations of a synthesis of the socialist-historical consciousness with individual freedom and toleration.

In the Soviet Union, since destalinization began, the tendency has been towards political and economic devolution, with greater toleration and greater room for the free play of individual liberty. But so far only the first steps in this direction have been taken. In the eighteenth century the crucial objective and historical question was: Enlightenment or *ancien régime* and Christianity? With the triumph of the bourgeoisie the question was transformed into a choice between bourgeois individualism and socialism. At this stage individualism came to seem an outdated phenomenon of history, while socialism appeared to be man's conscious assumption of responsibility for his historical mission. Today the question has taken an entirely new form.

The last forty years have faced us with the alternatives of a capitalist industrial society, which in providing the conditions for the progressive realization of the values of the Enlightenment simultaneously makes for ever greater spiritual emptiness, and a socialist industrial society, which gives content and scope for the development of an immanent humanist religion but once more threatens (or at any rate does not guarantee, as it was expected to do) the independence of the individual conscience, the great achievement of the Enlightenment. In objective historical terms, then, the question is still: Socialism or capitalism? But this question faces every Christian and every socialist with another which is vital to human intellectual life: Will western industrial society as it develops guarantee the values of *content* in intellectual life, or will the socialist form of society be able to develop into the guardian of the values of the Enlightenment: equality, freedom, toleration and the individual conscience of every one of its members?

If such a synthesis, for which mankind has striven since the Renaissance, can be attained, will the spiritual life of a genuinely transparent community be an immanent, historical and humanist religion or a more or less transcendental faith? This is a question to which at present there can be only more or less well supported subjective answers. As the reader will have guessed, I think the former outcome the more likely. But to offer this as a definitive answer would be to prophesy, and that is far from my purpose. A theorist is always standing at some particular point in historical development, and all he can do is to make earnest use of his critical powers in order to understand the problems of his times and express them in conceptual terms.

Index